More Praise for *Creating Time* and Marni

"When Marney's book arrived, I thought, 'Pshaw! There is no way to find more creative time.' It took maybe ten pages before I was rejoicing. Marney has done the impossible — created a plethora of joyful ways to transform how you see, experience, and create with time. This book is the time machine you've been waiting for."

— JENNIFER LOUDEN, author of *The Woman's Comfort Book* and *The Life Organizer*

"This book sails beyond time management into creating time, appreciating time, and replacing conditioned anxiety with magic. I never thought I'd experience joy in looking at time. But I felt expansive as I read this — tickled, curious, and loved. These right-brained techniques can help you uncover an exquisite abundance, even in your left-brained world."

— TAMA J. KIEVES, bestselling author of
This Time I Dance!: Creating the Work You Love, www.ThisTimeIDance.com

"If you've ever wished for more hours in a day (and who hasn't?), Marney Makridakis's magical book, *Creating Time*, is for you. Her wise insights, creative exercises, and inspiring artwork will empower you to say so long to scarcity and stress and hello to freedom, focus, and flow. Now, isn't it about time?"

— JENNIFER LEE, author of *The Right-Brain Business Plan*

"*Creating Time* is the magical and mirth-filled solution we've been waiting for to fit more of what we truly love into our lives. It brilliantly combines science, philosophy, and art in a whimsical package that is both practical and fun to read. I open it daily to remind me of my power to create time to be anything I want it to be."

— JILL BADONSKY, author of *The Awe-manac: A Daily Dose of Wonder*

"If time has become an obnoxious bully in your life, read Marney's beautiful book and you will discover dozens of creative ways to turn time into an uplifting guide. I particularly love her approach to intuiting the synchronicities in one's life and imagining time as a unified flow."

— SEENA B. FROST, founder of SoulCollage®, www.SoulCollage.com

"Imagine you had a wise and wonderful friend who could show you simple, yet artful and fun, ways to forever change your relationship with time. Wouldn't that just be the best gift ever? If you feel like you are always running out of time, if you feel the daily pressure and stress of 'not enough time,' this book will expand your mind, open your heart, and YES, give you all the time in the world."

— ARIELLE FORD, bestselling author of
Wabi Sabi Love: The Ancient Art of Finding Perfect Love in Imperfect Relationships

"In a society that seems to thrive on making us feel hurried and harried and pressed for time, this book stands firmly in the conviction that we have more time than we think we do and that we're entitled to every delicious minute of it. The farthest thing from a straitlaced 'time management book,' *Creating Time* is an artful collection of practical tips, creative exercises, and philosophic ponderings for making the most of every hour and, consequently, making the most of your life."

— VICTORIA MORAN, author of *Creating a Charmed Life*

CREATING TIME

CREATING TIME

Using Creativity to Reinvent the Clock and Reclaim Your Life

MARNEY K. MAKRIDAKIS

FOREWORD BY MARCI SHIMOFF

New World Library
Novato, California

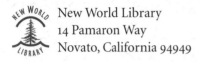

New World Library
14 Pamaron Way
Novato, California 94949

Text design by Tona Pearce Myers

Library of Congress Cataloging-in-Publication Data
Makridakis, Marney K., date.
 Creating time : using creativity to reinvent the clock and reclaim your life / Marney K. Makridakis ; foreword by Marci Shimoff.
    p.   cm.
ISBN 978-1-60868-111-2 (pbk. : alk. paper)
1. Time management. 2. Self-management (Psychology) 3. Creative ability. I. Title.
BF637.T5M25 2012
650.1'1—dc23   2012000883

First printing, April 2012
ISBN 978-1-60868-111-2
Printed in Canada on 100% postconsumer-waste recycled paper

New World Library is proud to be a Gold Certified Environmentally Responsible Publisher. Publisher certification awarded by Green Press Initiative. www.greenpressinitiative.org

10 9 8 7 6 5 4 3 2 1

Dedicated to my beloved timeline trio:

My father, Lonnie Kliever, in loving memory of the sacred past
My husband, Anthony Makridakis, in gratitude for the eternal present
My son, Kai Makridakis, in awe of the kaleidoscopic future

CONTENTS

SECTION 3: INTEGRATION AND INSPIRATION

FOREWORD

When I was starting my career, I thought success would be the golden ticket to everything in life. I imagined it would bring me freedom from the constraints of time and the stresses of overwhelm. Yet when I became a #1 *New York Times* bestselling author and met with the success I'd dreamed of, the challenges of *time* became even more pronounced.

I know I'm not alone. These days, everyone seems to be time challenged. When you ask people how they are, how often do you hear complaints like "I'm too busy," "I'm overwhelmed," or "I don't have enough time"?

It feels as though time has sped up over the past few years. More happens now in one month than used to happen in one year. New technology is supposed to help us increase our efficiency so that we can get more done, but instead we have become even greater slaves to time. We are falling farther behind as we struggle to fit everything into our already jam-packed days.

When I interviewed hundreds of people for my books, *Happy for No Reason* and *Love for No Reason*, trying to discover what makes them most fulfilled, I discovered that the people who are happiest and most love-filled have a unique relationship with time. They tend to be very present and fully engaged in the moment — they recognize the importance of "right now" and have mastered their relationship with "getting things done." Their healthy orientation to time leads to more fulfilling relationships, better health, and greater productivity.

During pivotal life moments, we often fall into an experience of "right now." At those special moments, we experience a state of fullness and true presence. But those glimpses are fleeting. Sustaining a lasting change in our relationship with time has always been difficult — until now. *Creating Time* offers tools that help us make the most of our most precious resource — time. Through the ARTsignments and creative play presented in this book, we can find liberation from our daily struggles with time, and we can discover we have all the time we need.

Creating Time is a heart-centered-yet-practical guide that offers a new paradigm of time and the tools to implement it. Marney Makridakis has devoted her career to helping people live fuller and more meaningful lives by connecting with their own creativity. In this unique and enchanting book, she shows us how to use our creativity to experience a new relationship with time. Marney's brilliant techniques combine art and philosophy, science and story, to help us connect deeply with the power of our creative selves. By accessing that part of our selves, we go beyond our normal ways of thinking and are able to experience time in more empowering ways.

So pull out your calendar, date book, and to-do list. With those close at hand, you can dive in to the bright, vivid pages that follow. You'll be guided to incorporate your *aha*s about your relationship with time directly into your life, creating a relationship that will have you wondering how you ever went about your days without the support of your new partner, time. Every step of the way, you'll be inspired by thought-provoking poetry and colorful art to stimulate your imagination and open you to profound insights. Through the power of your own imagination, you can create a new relationship with time and, as a result, feel more joyful, connected, aware, and alive. Enjoy your journey!

— MARCI SHIMOFF, *New York Times* bestselling author of
Happy for No Reason and *Love for No Reason*

INTRODUCTION

I began developing the material for this book shortly after giving birth to my son. I was thirty-seven years old, living a very full life largely focused on running a quickly growing online business. Like many new parents, I certainly was not prepared for the time involved in caring for an infant. Due to a long and difficult labor and delivery, shortly after giving birth I developed Bell's palsy, a neurological paralysis affecting one side of the face. Even after the paralysis reversed within a few months, I continued to feel *asymmetrical*, as I tried in vain to find the time to "do it all," fragmenting myself as I tried to play out all my roles. I was never fully present in anything I was doing, existing as a partial person as I exhaustively chased time.

After many months of soul-searching and dog-earing time management books, I found myself with a precious bit of quiet time at the beach, and I suddenly had the realization that human beings are forces of nature, constantly creating in the same way that the rolling tides of the ocean constantly create and re-create new worlds. Fueled by this new vision, I became determined to apply my best resource (imagination) to my biggest problem (time). I figured, since it is so hard to manage or save time, why not try to *create* it? As crazy as that sounded, I researched and experimented with imagining, viewing, and experiencing time in new ways, and I felt time expand and change at my design. I created an online course to help others do the same and saw that other people had success with these techniques as well. In short, I learned that when we don't have time, we have to create it…and we can do so using one of the greatest resources ever to exist on our planet: human creativity.

For most people, time is the biggest challenge in fulfilling their potential. Whatever improvements or changes we want to make in our lives, it often seems to go back to the topic of time; we need time to exercise and eat right, time to establish and strengthen relationships, time to pursue a meaningful hobby, time to follow a dream. We fantasize about adding ten hours to our days or taking ten years off our age. Our perceived lack of, and limitations on, time affect all areas of our lives, especially our hopes and dreams. Time is the ultimate scapegoat when things aren't going our way and also is the ultimate *resource* when we can learn how to control our perception of it. In just about every area of our life, it's somehow *all about time*.

We all think about and talk about time a lot, but do we really know what it means? Is time a dimension of the universe presenting itself as a thing or quality? Or is time a product of our consciousness that is merely a sensation or illusion? Our experiences of time are deeply ambiguous, if not downright paradoxical. I believe it is *because* time is so elusive that we can release the boundaries of its definition and redefine time to mean whatever we want it to mean. Through our creativity, we can reclaim time, transform it, and create it in our own design to be anything we want it to be. While we may not be able to literally expand the number of hours in a day and years in our lives, by expanding our *perception*, we can live each day in a time machine of sorts, traveling at our own tempo to destinations of our dreams.

The creative metamorphosis that you are about to embark upon in this book will guide you in discovering many unique ways to work with time — to rediscover it, feel it, perceive it, experience it, and step into it in entirely new ways. This book will give you tools with which to pause your rushing mind for a moment to connect with the intricate and fanciful work of art that you create each and every day, as you step into the full grandeur of possibility and wonder that time holds.

This book represents my journey from time management to time *metamorphosis*. Now you too can control your perception of time and experience it in a way that truly supports you and the highest vision of your life. Believe it or not, time *is* in your hands, and you can mold, craft, and create time to be just about anything you would like it to be.

Welcome to the adventure of a lifetime!

ABOUT THIS BOOK

Here is an overview of the book's structure and some useful features that will help you to make the most of your experience.

Section 1: Exploring Your Relationship with Time

The first section assists you in exploring your relationship with time, by both analyzing your present reality and exploring your deepest needs and desires. This section also provides a context for reinventing time, providing a useful framework for your adventures in the rest of the book.

Section 2: Creating Time through Creativity

The second section provides an inspiring collection of unique methods for *creating time through creativity*. Each chapter presents a specific concept, which is illustrated through supportive material such as personal stories and anecdotes, literary and fun pop culture references, and creative interpretations of scientific theory and evidence. Each chapter demonstrates, in a different way, that we can create time outside of a linear view and welcome a new way to experience time.

The conclusion of each chapter presents an "ARTsignment," which is an art project designed to activate and expand self-awareness and transformation. Each ARTsignment combines a step-by-step introspective process; interactive journal questions; and a unique, hands-on art project.

ARTsignments, which are at the core of my ARTbundance approach of self-discovery through creativity, offer a powerfully effective way to internalize and absorb a process and truly take it in. Through eight years of creating ARTsignments, I've discovered that engaging our minds, imaginations, and bodies through *physically creating art* catalyzes an unmistakable transition from simply reading a concept to *absorbing* and *becoming it*. Once understood,

> ### In a Hurry Hint
>
> If you picked up this book, there's a good chance that you are "in a hurry." If so, you may want to skip ahead to the Time Design Diagnosis Chart in chapter 15. You'll find a list of common time challenges and can select the ones most relevant to you, so that you can move directly to the sections you may find most helpful right now.

this method of essentially transporting oneself through creativity has very large and valuable implications regarding time "traveling" and time creation. In this book, ARTsignments pull us directly into the full dimensions of time and extend the breadth of its meaning and experience.

When you approach the ARTsignments, please remember that these projects are not about demonstrating artistic skill or ability, or about creating artistic masterpieces. They are about using creativity as a conduit for exploration. In ARTsignments, the emphasis is completely on the process rather than the product, and this holds true whether you are sketching stick figures on a paper napkin, making a collage of magazine cutouts, painting on a canvas, or creating an elaborate mixed media sculpture. The beauty of ARTsignments is that *anyone* can do them; you don't need to be an "artist" to tap into the transformative power of creativity. In this book, you'll see examples of ARTsignments created by ARTbundance Coaches and Practitioners, as well as their clients and students, who collectively represent a wide range of people from a variety of artistic and personal backgrounds. Their examples are intended to inspire more ideas and new directions for your own ARTsignment creations.

My team and I facilitate an ARTbundance Certification Training Program (ACT), in which trainees learn how to use the ARTbundance Principles and ARTsignments in professional venues, such as creativity coaching, public speaking, teaching, leading workshops, and creating online learning environments. For more information about ARTbundance and ACT, you can visit the web page: ArtellaLand.com/ACT.html

Section 3: Integration and Inspiration

The final section presents processes to integrate all of the time creation concepts into *your* real life. The Time Design Diagnosis Chart helps you to determine which techniques in this book may be helpful to you and how you might implement them in your daily experience. Additional practical tools and processes are introduced to guide you to examine your own schedule and circumstances to personalize the ways that you experience time to help you to feel more free and alive, every single moment, every single day.

Poetic Pauses

Each chapter begins with a *poetic pause* — a short haiku that explores time through a metaphorical lens. I selected the traditional haiku format (three lines with a specific syllabic structure: five syllables, seven syllables, then five syllables) as an exercise in awareness of the role of *timing* in words and phrases. These short pieces have several purposes: First, they encourage you to change the pace and timing at which you read, inviting you to slow your reading as you meditate and reflect on the image presented. They also offer a gift of *pausability*, as you grasp your ability to pause and alter your timing, combined with a moment of *possibility*, as you open to seeing time in a new way through the metaphor presented.

As you read each poem, I invite you to extend the moment even further and reflect on its meaning not only in this moment but *through* time. For example:

- What does the poem make you remember? (past)
- How does the poem make you feel right now? (present)
- What wishes or dreams come to mind? (future)

I also encourage you to compose your own poetic pauses, perhaps even jotting them in the margins of the book. This is a powerful device to prompt you to pause and absorb what you are reading, and to translate it into your own experience.

SECTION 1

EXPLORING YOUR RELATIONSHIP WITH TIME

1. WHAT IS TIME?

Poetic Pause

Time as sunflowers
Facing the light in worship
Petaling forward

T he subject of time covers everything from how long something takes to how old we are, how long we will live, and decisions about the "right time" to make choices or take action. Time is familiar to everyone, and yet it's quite challenging to define and identify.

Modern science defines time within the term *space-time* in an effort to explain that coordinates in time do not exist without the corresponding coordinates in space. Space-time may therefore reference a scientific interpretation of time. To fully explain the personal experience of time, however, there are an endless number of "coordinates" that locate us in a certain moment, such as emotions, expectations, relationships, and values.

We do not live in purely sequential time, where any moment consists of the moment and that moment only. In fact, the true "present" is so brief that it can't even be perceived. So, naturally, even when we are completely focused in the present, our awareness extends both to the past and to the future. To illustrate the brief temporality of the present, Leonardo da Vinci said, "The water you touch in a river is the last of that which has passed, and the first of that which is coming. Thus it is with time present."

The term *specious present*, coined by E. Robert Kelly (aka E. R. Clay) in 1882, refers to the period that we tend to think of as the present, though it also includes the near past and upcoming future. Specious present indicates the overlap between the circles of past, present, and future. In actuality, though, our perception extends beyond the overlap of three defined circles. We can feel the fabric of time folding itself over us, or perhaps folding itself *within* us, at every given moment.

> *"I have a vision of the three bears with bowls of 'time' instead of porridge. Ultimately, time is precious, whether it's going too fast, too slow, or just right."*
>
> — SANDE ROBERTS,
> ARTbundance Coach

By way of example, I identified a few of the time continua that we use to measure and define time, and asked artist Michelle Berlin to illustrate them as linear timelines. As you can see, each one is represented here by an arrow facing in one direction.

Ink on paper, 7 x 7.5 in.

THE SCIENTIFIC CONTINUUM
Order   TO   DISORDER

THE LINEAR CONTINUUM
Past   PRESENT   Future

THE NARRATIVE CONTINUUM
Beginning   MIDDLE   END

THE PERCEPTION CONTINUUM
TIME MOVES Slow   TO   Fast

THE AGING CONTINUUM
YOUNG   TO   Old

Linear Time Continua
by Michelle Berlin

The *Linear Time Continua* graphs indicate a variety of *quantitative* continua. However, *qualitative* continua are more multidimensional, allowing us to measure time in an infinite number of ways. Here are some examples that come to my mind, again illustrated by Michelle:

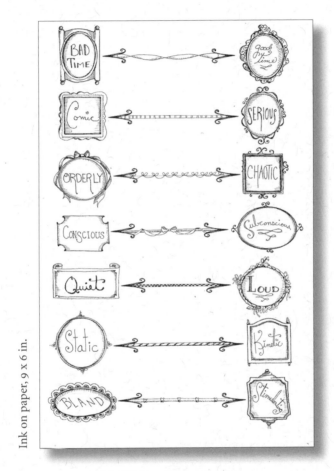

Ink on paper, 9 x 6 in.

Nonlinear Time Continua
by Michelle Berlin

Any given moment can be plotted on any combination of the above timelines, as a way to "measure" it. However, when we do so, the measurement consists not only of the "dot" itself but also of the very continuum it lies upon. No matter how we choose to measure time, any moment includes the *entire* time continuum. Time is not something outside of us; it is an element of everything.

THE PROBLEM WITH TIME

I asked some ACT trainees why we have time, and here are a few of their responses:

"Time allows us to see, to witness the unfolding of free will." — Tanya Laurin

"We use time to categorize our moments, by year, era, or timeline. Time is a backdrop to place our memories in order, to make sense of the happenings that take us from here to there." — Amy Heil

"Time makes life's 'little gifts' bigger. Time is here for us to learn and heal and discover." — Peggy Lynn

As all the statements above indicate, the structure of time allows us to see and experience life. And yet time also can blind us to greater truths, as our time-based consciousness can greatly limit our worldview.

The concept of *time management* is very new, just as "stress" is a modern phenomenon. Time management can improve what we *accomplish* but often at the peril of what we *experience*. As a result, the more we try to manage our time, the more fragmented we feel. If you pay attention to the conversations all around you, it's startling how often the subject of time comes up.

"How are you?"
"Oh fine, just crazy busy…"

"You should come check it out…"
"Yeah, I know; I just don't know when I can find the time…"

"How are you?"
"I can't really talk now, I'm running late…"

People used to be tied to things like families, communities, rituals, worship, curiosity, and beauty. Now we are tied to schedules, watches, datebooks, computers, gadgets that start with *i*, the media, and exercising on treadmills that don't go anywhere.

ARTbundance Coach Amy Heil expressed it nicely: "When we become a slave to the system of measuring time, when we are focused on too much or not enough, we are not serving our best interests. This instant is truly endangered, so the only time to focus on is now!"

Somehow the tendencies of our society make it acceptable and even expected that we fall into patterns of being worried and stressed about time. And while worrying about time seems to be part of our humanity, I wonder…does it really need to be?

Time Collage by Patricia J. Mosca

Acrylic and watercolor on paper, 6 x 8 in.

MEASUREMENT AND PERCEPTION

One second is officially defined in atomic time as 9,192,631,770 oscillations of the "undisturbed" cesium atom. However, even with this precise number of oscillations, time is surprisingly nonuniform. There is *not* perfect unity between the rotation of the earth (which measures a day) and atomic time. In fact, official time often has to be put back or forward a bit to compensate.

We measure time in a variety of units, from seconds, hours, and minutes to beginning, middle, end. We also measure time according to our needs ("Is it time to eat yet?"), external demands ("When is it due?"), and anticipations ("Are we there yet?"). Regardless of how we measure time, however, that measurement is always trumped by perception. While so many of us are controlled by time, the interesting thing is that we're rarely aware of time itself. We usually don't know how long something takes in the moment, and yet its length is how we end up measuring it.

I was stunned at my own inability to correctly perceive time when recently I was having an MRI and was situated so that I could see a countdown timer of the scan, which I presume is there so that the patient knows how much longer she needs to stay still. I played a game of closing my eyes and opening them when I thought a minute had passed. The first time, I opened my eyes after only forty seconds. I tried again, and it had been forty-one seconds. I continued to try for each minute, and each time I was "accurate" within my own perception: I always opened my eyes at around forty seconds. It was only when I pushed myself to wait a little longer that I came closer to a minute, and I was still under sixty seconds.

Naturally, lying still in an MRI machine would qualify as one of those instances when time perception is slowed, the antithesis of "Time flies when you're having fun." Still, I was surprised at my experience. I suppose I shouldn't have been; many scientific experiments have proved that individuals have a varying sense of perception of time passing. *Psychochronometry* is the study of the psychology of time estimation. Many studies have explored the various factors that affect time perception, including environment, emotions, and age. Studies of the Logtime Hypothesis, for example, have found that perception of the passage of time increases by the square root of one's age, and at age sixty, time is perceived about two and a half times faster than it was at age ten.

I decided to conduct my own experiment, a casual way of estimating time perception during a creative activity. I asked fifty-two people to create a *word collage* for what they perceived to be one minute. Here are the instructions they were given; I invite you to try this yourself.

1. Grab a piece of paper and a marker or colored pen, and have a clock or watch with a second hand nearby.
2. Without looking at the timer/clock, create a word collage on the topic of time for what you think is one minute. Note the time when you begin, and start when the second hand is on the 12, so that you can easily track your timing.

3. Create a word collage by filling the page with all the words you think of when you think about time. Do not look at the clock, count, or use any other way to keep track of your timing.

4. When you intuitively think that one minute has passed, check the clock and make note of your *actual* time.

Word collage examples by, clockwise from top left:
Peggy Lynn, TiCo, Vivian Sakellariou, Rae Shagalov, Chris Hammer

The following pie chart illustrates the results:

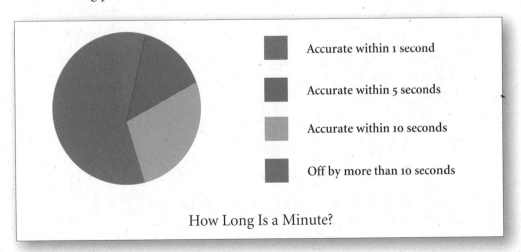

Accurate within 1 second

Accurate within 5 seconds

Accurate within 10 seconds

Off by more than 10 seconds

How Long Is a Minute?

As these results show, the vast majority were off by a significant amount: 54 percent were off by more than ten seconds. One look at the extremes on the chart gives a good idea of how differently "one minute" is perceived!

Here are a few of the comments of the individuals who completed the exercise:

"This minute went really fast. It's funny to compare that with the 'slow speed' of a watched minute."

"It took twice as long as I intended. I think this correlates to the many times when it takes twice as long to do something than what my optimistic nature anticipates."

"I felt rushed because I knew I only had a minute, and was surprised that I stopped so early, so I actually had more time left than I thought."

Interestingly, we are unaware of not only the time itself but also the very effect that time has on us. For example, we've all had the experience of seeing someone that we haven't seen in years and remarking at how much the person has changed. Yet physical changes are almost imperceptible in people we live with or see every day.

Mixed media on cardboard box, 8 x 10 x 2 in.

Time Box by Janet Shepherd

Why are we so obsessed with ordering our lives around something we can't even accurately perceive? Perhaps it's our attempt to create order out of the apparent chaos of our lives on this planet. If so, then as far as human evolution has brought us, especially in the past few decades, we would be well served to incorporate new, fresh measuring tools for the ever-more-important concept of time.

Given the inconsistency in our perception of time, it's no wonder, then, that we are anxious about time. The discrepancy between the extent to which measured time controls our lives and the actual abstract quality of time leads to an inherent disconnect. I experienced this profoundly when I followed a bit of time management advice and recorded a time estimate beside each item in my daily to-do list (for example, call to schedule appointment — five minutes; write an article — one hour; and so on). As the book predicted, this did in fact increase my productivity and effectiveness. Even more staggering, however, was what I uncovered when I reevaluated my past daily lists using this criterion. When I went back to recent daily lists and applied time estimates to the tasks I had put on my lists, I realized that I had been expecting myself to do as much as thirty hours of tasks in a single workday. This  discovery was life changing for me. No wonder I always felt like there wasn't enough time. No wonder each and every day had a gauzy sense of failure around it. My perception of "the time in the day" was so unrealistic that I was constantly filled with a deep sense of lack and overwhelm.

Of course, being overwhelmed about time leads to feeling overwhelmed about the things we *do* with time: not only our responsibilities and commitments but also our opportunities, projects, ideas, and dreams. This is why so many people stop themselves from pursuing a goal with a simple catchall excuse: "There's not enough time." Ironically, when I looked at time in a more limited way (that is, I became more aware of how much time my tasks actually took), I was opened to a more *expansive* view of time. I realized how attuned I had become to a perceived lack of time. Time is a valuable resource that is far more infinite than we tend to think it is. We worry so much about not having enough time, when time is, in fact, one resource that is always present, for as long as we are living. Much like oxygen, time is there for us. While the finite amount of time we have is real, the occasions when we *feel* it lacking, drifting, or lost are largely a matter of perception only.

It's a human paradox, because we often want to escape ourselves and lose track of time, and yet it is when we become fully aware of the gift of time that we become more present and in touch. I believe that a solution lies in the state in which we become less aware of time but *more aware of the present moment*. What we need are more tools to support this blissful state.

TIME-KEEPING ALTERNATIVES

We measure time in linear fashion, with numbers on a clock and squares on a calendar to represent the forward arrow of time. But what if we could interpret time as a qualitative entity instead of something just measured by quantity? For example, instead of measuring how *long* something takes, why not measure it by how much we *learn* by doing it? We might experiment with forgoing a measurement of minutes and instead think about how much we can be *in it*. How deeply can you extend your awareness to be truly present, conscious, and connected to everything around you right now? What effect does this extension of meaning have on time?

Of course we traditionally think of time as quantitative. We know how long something takes. We know when our deadlines are. We know what time we have to show up at the appointment. Yet if we allow ourselves to think about time *qualitatively*, then we open up opportunities to measure time by something less arbitrary, and far more meaningful, than cesium I-23 atoms.

This shift is actually something we have all experienced before. Think about the moments in your life that have meant the most to you. Those moments are not viewed linearly at all, but through a plethora of other measurements, such as intensity of experience, emotional depth, and even quality of color or the particular scent of the moment. Our minds seem to automatically assign nonlinear associations to the "important times." We can learn from these experiences by applying a similar free-form perception in our everyday moments.

For example, instead of measuring how long something takes, why not measure it by things like:

- How much you learn
- How much joy you feel
- How relaxed you feel
- How connected you are to your passion

- How much you are affected by another person
- How "right" you feel

Incorporating these new "measurements" doesn't mean that we are forgoing the linear methods entirely. Rather, we are aware of both kinds of time, but it is the qualitative measurements that are, in the long run, more important. Our sleeping hours are a great example of this duality. Most of us would prefer to get six hours of deep, restful sleep rather than nine hours of tossing and turning. While we can be aware of the number of hours we sleep and even plan our schedule to ensure that we sleep a certain number of hours, we are far more focused on the quality of the sleep that we have achieved. Similarly, when evaluating our time, we can be aware of the hours and minutes passed, but the quality of those moments is what really matters.

This book presents new time-tracking alternatives and invites you to try different mechanisms and media for measuring time. The mind-sets and tools presented are both practical and philosophical. On the practical level, this book will help you to make tangible choices and changes about how you use and perceive time, while on the philosophical level, the tools are geared to work deeply within, unearthing new, uplifting beliefs and ideas about time and life itself.

ARTsignment: ARTernity Box

This book will guide you to create time to be anything you want it to be: to feel it, experience it, and use it in ways that improve your life. You'll discover your own inner eternity as you use creativity to design new visions and expansions of time. But before you venture into new time territory, it's helpful to examine your current relationship with time. For this project, you'll be examining your beliefs about time as you create a special ARTernity Box that provides a holding place for these beliefs.

Step 1: Your first step is to gather your supplies to create your ARTernity Box: a box or container decorated in a time motif. It can be any shape or size, provided that it can hold several slips of paper. You can create your box using any supplies or media that you like — ideally, supplies that you have on hand. For inspiration and ideas, refer to the ARTsignment Gallery below.

Step 2: Begin working on your box. As you work, reflect on your thoughts and feelings about time. Often, having our hands busy, such as when creating art, allows our minds to open and thoughts to flow more freely. So just relax and allow your mind to wander freely on the subject of time. Feel free to incorporate into the design of the box any thoughts, feelings, or images that come to mind.

Step 3: When the box is complete, gather some small pieces of paper and a pen. Answer each of the following questions on a different slip of paper.

1. When you think about time, what is the first thing that comes to mind?
2. What is your deepest wish, regarding time?
3. What is your biggest challenge, regarding time?
4. Do you spend more time wishing time would speed up or go more slowly? Why?
5. If you had more time, how might your life be different?
6. If you knew you had less time on this earth, how might your life be different?
7. If you suddenly never had to worry about time, how might your life be different?
8. What methods have you used to keep track of your time (calendars, smartphones, online calendars, datebooks, and so on)? Which methods work best for you? Which seem to be least effective?
9. Do you wear a watch? Why or why not?
10. What was "time" like in your house when you were growing up? What

beliefs did your parents and/or other family members have about time, and how were those beliefs manifested in their actions?

11. How is your current experience of time related to these patterns and observations from your childhood?

12. What drew you to this book?

Step 4: Put the slips in your ARTernity Box, where they will be held safely in a time capsule as you travel through your own creative inner eternity.

ARTsignment Gallery: ARTernity Box

Mixed media assemblage, 5.5 x 10 x 3 in.

"The ARTernity Box I made was based on an old camera case. This is a reminder that I get to capture each precious snapshot in my life. Doing this ARTsignment made me realize that I really had more time to be creative, but I had just not been using it. I have to remind myself that I am *allowed* to take the time to be creative. After all, one day we will all be at the point of dying and we will be saddened at all of the time we let slip away that we weren't truly enjoying. This project helped me remember to do what I am being called to do creatively." — ANGELA BYERS

ARTSIGNMENT GALLERY: ARTERNITY BOX

Collage on cardboard canister, 13 x 4 in.

"To contain my thoughts about time, I made my own 'time in a bottle.' I always liked the song by Jim Croce, and so I was inspired to use a wine canister that I received as a gift. I covered it with a sunny scrapbooking paper and magazine cutouts of watches and sundials. The pictures of jewels on the container represented special moments to me. The scene of the cottage in the country garden made me think of the long lazy summer days of my youth when time stretched on and on. Doing this reminded me that there is always time for the most important things."

— MARY BUTTERFIELD BROSHEAR

ARTsignment Gallery: ARTernity Box

Collage on wooden box, 7.5 x 9.5 x 6.75 in.

"Creating this box helped me see that I always have time for my art, and to do it my way. I used photos, pictures, and embellishments to create my piece, and it was very freeing. I now take the time to create, and do it in 'my' style."   — GERRIE JOHNNIC

ARTSIGNMENT GALLERY: ARTERNITY BOX

Woodcut designs on cardboard box, 5 x 4.5 x 4.5 in.

"The inspiration for my ARTernity Box was a woodcut I carved several years ago, with a circular design that suggests a clock. I slightly altered the image, made copies, and covered each side of a tissue box cube with a different clock face, representing four different ways that I track time: hours in my day, days in my week, months in my year, and decades in my life. The angel figure represents my creative self, living simultaneously within these different time modes. Making the ARTernity Box reminded me of how happily absorbed I am when creating, so I have placed the box in a prominent spot in my workroom to encourage me to include and embrace more creativity in my hours, days, months, and decades for the rest of my life."

— ARTHISS KLIEVER

2. YOUR RELATIONSHIP WITH TIME

Poetic Pause

Time as strong embrace
Enveloping a deep wish
Whispering secrets

Scientifically speaking, time is simply the presence of motion and forces. Psychologically speaking, time is the perception of temporal experience. Personally speaking, time is simply *yours*: whatever it is and whatever you want it to be. Time is so personal, so much a part of us, that it can never be a "thing" that we measure, stop, save, chase, or — heaven forbid — kill. Time exists *inclusive of our feelings about it*.

All three states of time — past, present, and future — affect our feelings about time. First, our childhood experiences with time play a large role in our current relationship with time. I grew up in a household very much driven by time. My mother ran a detailed, highly planned household, and my father arrived at least fifteen minutes early no matter where he went. I'm now married to a man with a more flexible approach to time, not to mention living with a toddler who has no sense of time at all! Thus, my past and present temporal environments are strikingly different from one another. My expectation for orderly time often conflicts with the more unpredictable time in my reality, and I get more upset about plans and schedules than I'd like to.

Here are a few other examples that illustrate the influence of childhood experiences with time. Violette Clark, an artist and author, recalled,

My parents did not believe we should have too much idle time on our hands. They were pretty strict. As a result, I think I procrastinate. I overcompensate by wasting precious time. There has to be a happy medium somewhere! My folks also believed that you had to work hard to get anywhere in life, and I was taught how to be obedient and to say yes to requests. As a result, I have difficulty saying no and taking time for myself.

ARTbundance Coach Amy Heil shared, "When I was a kid, my mom had every clock set to a different time. The kitchen clock was always ten minutes fast. Time was twenty-five minutes fast on her alarm clock next to the bed. When we got a VCR and a microwave, they too had some random calculation of time. I find this interesting now, because I feel helpless when I cannot control time. But truly, no one can."

TiCo, an artist and ARTbundance Coach, can identify that her guilt over indulging in "nothing time" comes from childhood: "It was considered 'lazy' back then, but now I thrive on empty time to create ideas." Similarly, Bill Charlebois identified guilt as a big component of his current challenges with time: "There was definitely worry in our family about both the past and the future. There was too much guilt always being forced upon us. Having been raised by an abusive father, I now have difficulty feeling worthy enough to handle many present relationships and assignments. I worry about failure a lot, and this definitely affects time."

> "Sometimes I feel like I have to be busier and move faster to outrun the feeling that I am avoiding the 'real work' of being still."
>
> — SHEILA MASSON,
> ARTbundance Coach

Similarly, the ideals we place on our *future* time, in the form of our hopes and dreams and expectations, reverberate into our overall perception of time. When I was intently focused on losing weight, the time couldn't seem to pass quickly enough. I was very connected to my goal and felt I would reach it, yet I wanted time to just "hurry up already" so that I could get there. My preoccupation with my future definitely inhibited my ability to fully *inhabit* the present moment.

Time is so personal to each of us, and yet we are all expected to keep and follow the same chronological time. Releasing our tethers to sequential, linear time allows us to fully personalize time, the time that is truly ours. We can dance with it, sing with it, and even become it ourselves.

Creativity is a wonderful conduit to explore our personal relationship with time. A great place to start is to write a poem about time by filling in the blanks with any words that come to mind:

Time is _____
Time is _____
Time is _____
Time is _____
Time is _____

This exercise is an effective way to instantly get a sense of time's meaning to you right now. What do you see from your words? Are there any surprises? Are the words mostly positive or negative, harmonious or opposing?

Collage on chipboard, 10 x 8 in.

Time Guide by Gerrie Johnnic

A Snapshot of Time

time is paint that always looks wet
dreams that fall on the ground
and pierce the cobblestones with their spears
    of hope

time is sleepy roses
lines that actors remember
words that people can't forget

time is a screw sighing into cement
on a highway covered with quilts of cars with
    clocks
thoughts of being too late sideswipe
    regrets of being too old
time is cake batter that may have been baked
    or not
lies that became truths
truths forgotten in the cusps of orchids
whose beauty is less painful to
    remember

time is finding a nest and waiting past dark
    for the family to return
finally, one single feather comes back
its weight breaks the branch and the nest
    crashes
gone

time is half a breath when you say
    good-bye
forty thousand breaths as you wait to come
    home

Your poem is a slice of time, a representation of time's meaning right now. Since our present circumstances change so quickly, our impressions and experiences with time are constantly changing as well. Artella, the company that I founded ten years ago, began as a hobby to self-publish a magazine celebrating collaborations between artists and writers. The very first issue, printed on my desktop printer in 2002, was called *Time: When Kronos and Kairos Kiss*. I wrote a poem for that issue about time (see the sidebar "A Snapshot of Time"), and through the symbolic references in the poem, I can instantly recall things happening in my life then. It's a clear snapshot of my relationship *with* time, *in* time.

We might learn much about ourselves by simply repeating the poem-writing exercise at regular intervals to explore our ever-changing relationship with time. What would we learn if we had a quick time-slice poem to mark each month, or each year? I see this exercise as a tangible way to keep "time in a bottle" and underline the power of perception in time, while also owning our control of this perception.

WHAT DO YOU NEED FROM TIME?

To ask more from time, and from ourselves, the first step is to identify what it is that we personally need from time. Identifying our most significant time needs begins expanding our awareness. You can "tell time" by literally *telling time* what you need. Take a look at the sidebar "Telling Time What We Need" to get some ideas.

One of the most common desires is to have time that is "managed": time that is efficient and productive. In addition to efficient time, we also need other types of time, including:

- Dream time
- Creative time
- Nothing time
- Concentrated time
- Expansive time
- Self-care time
- Relationship time
- Private time
- Family time
- Rest time
- Planning/preparation time
- Spiritual/sacred time

What other kinds of time do you need? Which of these "times" are most important to you right now? What do you *really* need from time?

Worrying about Time

Try this: Imagine who you would be if you didn't worry about time. How might your life be different? I surveyed fifty-two people, and the results revealed that 90 percent felt "somewhat anxious" to "significantly anxious" about time. What's even more startling is that these results don't even seem all that surprising. Anxiety about time is very much a part of most of our lives. Think back to a time when you

Telling Time What We Need

Here are some of the things that participants in a recent workshop shared that they need from time:

"When I find the time to do what I want, I have no energy left. I'm just exhausted, and yet I feel guilty for not using the time better. I'm just sitting in front of the TV, not really watching it. I'm wasting the time I do have, so I end up feeling that there's not enough time."

"There's so much I want to do, and it feels like there's not enough time to make it happen. I'd like to have more trust that time really is on my side."

"I've been a mother and housewife for thirty years, and now I feel like it's finally time for me, and I don't even know what that means. I feel like I've put my whole life toward taking care of others and there is nothing to show for it. I feel like time has just passed me by."

"I actually feel like I have too much time on my hands; sometimes I don't know how to fill it. I don't know what's most important and where my time should go."

"I don't make time for what's most important. It feels like in order to make time for me, I have to take it from somewhere else, and I don't have anyplace else to take it from."

greeted a casual acquaintance and asked how he was, and he said, "Great! Things are fantastic!" It can be almost jarring when someone responds so positively. Somehow we're more conditioned to expect to hear people complain that they are tired, or sigh that they are busy.

It's helpful to dig deeply to figure out what is at the root of our problems with time. Why do we overschedule ourselves? Why do we want to be so busy? Why are we so consumed with time? Why does it seem so "normal" to worry about time so much? Why is it easier to be caught up in a drama about time than it is to be re-leased from it?

In short, what is the *payoff* for worrying about time?

When I examine this question myself, I can recognize that the more I complain about time, the more I block my ability to accept and express love and connection. Violette Clark shared, "I suppose not having enough time, or the illusion of believing this, makes us feel important. I also realize it keeps me safe. There have been a lot of dreams that I've accomplished, including publishing a book, but there have been a lot of balls that I've dropped, too, in the name of 'not having enough time.' Putting myself out there more fully means more potential for rejection. Sometimes not 'going for my dreams' is safer."

Similarly, artist Peggy Lynn boldly admitted that time complaints are related to ego: "The 'I'm too busy' implication does stroke the ego: 'Oh, look at me — busy, busy, busy!'" A workshop participant shared that her worries about time give her an excuse and an outside source for not following her dreams. She said, "I've never been someone who likes to blame, but now I suddenly realize that I've actually been blaming time. I don't have enough time, and so that's why I don't go after this dream, or that's why I haven't tried this or followed up on that. Then it's not my fault. This was a big discovery for me!"

Here are some examples of payoffs that people might receive from worrying or complaining about time:

- Time is a good catchall: if I can complain about being busy, then I don't have to look at other areas in my life.
- Worrying about time gives me something to talk about with other people.
- Worrying about time is a convenient excuse for not following my dreams.

- My schedule is wrapped up with my self-esteem. Being "too busy" means that I'm successful.
- I don't plan things that I might enjoy because it is too scary — it just feels safer to be bored.

Do any other payoffs come to mind? Which ones resonate as possibly being true for you? For further reflection, refer to the questions in the sidebar "Exploring Your Time Anxiety."

Once we can identify the payoffs that we get from worrying about time, we can see them for what they are: illusions that keep us from living our true potential. Simply being aware of what we are getting from our time worries allows us to make a different choice. Choice is one of the nine ARTbundance Principles, which are building blocks to self-awareness. Making new choices is one of the best ways we can explore new layers of freedom with time. Dana Sebastian-Duncan, a trainee in the ACT program, put it nicely: "When I really think of the Principle of Choice as it relates to time, it reminds me that I have the freedom to create my life and my own 'reality.' My daily choices add up to my life, and that is empowering."

Exploring Your Time Anxiety

To discover new insights about the roots of your time anxiety, try exploring these questions by writing your answers in your journal:

1. What are your biggest complaints, worries, or anxieties about time?
2. When you were growing up, what did you observe about time, schedules, busyness, and stillness? What did your parents and other family members believe about these things? How do those beliefs influence your life today?
3. How do you feel about your age? Do you worry or complain about being too old or too young?
4. What do you get from having these worries? How do these complaints or worries help you? You can refer to the payoffs described in this section for ideas.

TIME AND BALANCE

One of the most prevalent comments I've heard about time is the idea that we need to balance our time to live a more "balanced" life. I think the concept of balance is, sadly, often misunderstood. We often feel that if we are focused and disciplined, upbeat and positive, loving and generous, healthy and energetic…then we will be

Mixed media collage on cardboard, 8 x 6 in.

My Time Muse by Mary Butterfield Broshear

"balanced people." And if the pie chart of our daily life has just the right ratios of work, life, family, health, spirituality, and service, then our time will be "balanced."

This belief contains several fallacies. First, as we are breathing human beings, it's unfortunately impossible to have everything balanced all the time. If we are always striving for something that is inherently unattainable, we're sure to end up feeling like failures, because we'll never, ever feel good enough. When we can get rid of the false ideals, however, and instead just expect and *enjoy* the chaotic, off-kilter, asymmetrical essence of life, it opens us up to a great deal of freedom, which is instrumental to greater success in any projects we're undertaking.

The problem with striving for balance is that most people's understanding of this state swerves away from what balance actually is! Balance is not about walking around with a bunch of "positive," happy qualities; it's about walking the tightrope between the poles within us and the circumstances outside of us. It's taken me a while, but I've learned that true balance, ironically, means that we accept the parts of ourselves that can be pretty lopsided. Balance means we can embrace and love the most topsy-turvy parts because they offer gifts for full, authentic living. A certain amount of chaos in both space and time is often powerful fuel for creative people. The trick is to find the ways that the chaos of time can infuse our work and, in turn, how our work can energize our time.

Even though we measure time in a linear way, time is and always will be asymmetrical. One moment is not like another, just as each day is different and each tide that rolls in is different from the next. This is why it is impossible to "balance our time" by some objective pie-chart formula in a time management book. Exploring nonlinear, asymmetrical time allows us to *move in tandem* with an inherently lopsided time and thus regain our relative balance. If we stop constantly measuring ourselves against the standards of linear time, we can accept ourselves more fully. New possibilities emerge as we tango with tenacity and disco with uncertainty.

TRUSTING TIME

The term *divine timing* typically refers to the idea that everything happens at the "right" time. In spite of its label, I believe this concept to exist independent of religious or spiritual beliefs. Regardless of our beliefs, we all can benefit from remembering that life's mysteries preclude our intellectual understanding of why and when things happen. We have all had experiences of wanting something to happen and being devastated when it didn't, only to realize later that "the timing wasn't right." Whether you believe that events in our lives are guided by a higher power or you simply believe in the mystery of what can never be fully known about life, divine timing is a concept that can provide assurance, comfort, and freedom.

Divine timing plays a significant role in the training sessions I run. For example, ACT trainees are given weekly assignments, but they are given the freedom to submit

> *"Divine time allows the answers to show up when they're ready to show up. If I were left to figure out how to breathe, how to create a baby, how to make a heart beat, digest food, or pulse blood in this fragile body system, I know I'd mess that up. These things work themselves to perfection without our help, and I do believe that when we're aligned with our purpose, timing works for us in the same way."*
>
> — TiCo, ARTbundance Coach

their work whenever they want…in divine timing. This approach releases the trainees from the external pressures of creating by a deadline and teaches them to follow their own clock. In a few instances, perhaps the emphasis on divine timing has provided an excuse for procrastination, but this happens far less often than one might think. Ironically, I've found that more assignments get completed "on time" when the outside due date is released. Far more important, the *quality* of both the process and the product is significantly improved, as trainees feel the freedom to take the time they need, without being limited by artificial, external pressures.

Gifts of Divine Timing

Divine timing allows us to:

*   Be gentle with ourselves
*   Be forgiving of others
*   Welcome new layers of meaning in unexpected events
*   Embrace life's mysteries
*   Align with nonlinear time
*   Open awareness to new opportunities
*   Transition more swiftly through disappointment
*   Develop faith
*   Practice resilience
*   Bring forward our best selves
*   Trust the very process of our lives

As we become more trusting of divine timing, we can call upon it at our will. Rae Shagalov expressed it nicely: "When I am in a hurry, I often pause in the midst of my anxious rush and pretend that I have all the time in the world. I stop, move slowly, do something extra, think more slowly and luxuriously, and remember that all timing is divine timing and happens exactly the way it is supposed to happen."

For some people, trusting in divine timing comes naturally, as it is synonymous with trusting God or a higher power. Others may find it easier to relate to the concept of divine timing by trusting *time* itself. My friend Susan Kennedy, known in her books and artwork as SARK, expressed her views on divine timing:

We, as humans, are not "in charge" of time the way we often think we are. There are spiritual dimensions of time that are always in effect. One of my favorite examples of this is when we say something happened "out of the blue." The "blue" knows what's coming, but we don't know. We think we can predict, forecast, or control time, and to a certain extent, it appears to work, but allowing divine timing is a far more powerful force. I've experienced this countless times as I've tried to "make something happen" by a certain date or time, and then let go and watched as divine timing worked its magic.

It is helpful to personify the entity of time and realize that we can build trust in time, just as we build trust in people: through an ongoing relationship sustained by exploration, awareness, dialogue, and evidence. To facilitate a deeper trust in time, the ARTsignment at the end of this chapter leads you to create a Time Guide to help cultivate a relationship with time in a personified form. Your Time Guide is an imaginary persona that you create, a benevolent figure who supports you fully and gives you exactly what you need in the area of time. The more deeply you give yourself over to getting to know this new persona, the more you'll find yourself trusting time and feeling more comfortable with it.

When you create your Time Guide, you may find that the form of the persona brings you surprising realizations. Gerrie Johnnic had a startling insight when she caught a glimpse of her Time Guide in progress on the table in her craft room. She said, "I noticed this figure was sitting on top of this huge pile of stuff. And I realized that it was *me*. This is my life right now: I have a mess all around me, and I

Peggy's Story: Divine Time Personified

Acrylic on paper, 12 x 9 in.

Divine Mother by Peggy Lynn

"My Time Guide is the Divine Mother. The idea came to me instantly — of course! She would remain at my side forever, because she is always there. I can call upon her beauty, wisdom, and grace not just by my side but permeating my soul, as a beloved companion. As I created her, I was aware of her total unconditional love for everything, because she is a nurturer! This is exactly what I need from time. We journaled back and forth for days. One thing she said in a letter to me was, 'The time is right for your strong hands and my strong hands to intertwine like a fine tapestry. Where I am carrying the world beckoning you and others, you have the world in the palms of your hands. Use it or lose it! I want you to use it! It is time for you to come out of the shadows and do so!'"   — Peggy Lynn need to un-mess my life and feel free. My Time Guide doesn't seem bothered by the mess, though, so maybe I can learn from her!"

The next step of the ARTsignment is to converse with your Time Guide, through the time-honored tradition of letter writing. This exercise allows you to intimately study your relationship with time and begin to transform it. If you are new to the idea of dialoguing with inanimate personas, it may take a while to get used to it. I encourage you to stick with it, because the results can be quite powerful, as you become more comfortable "channeling" your Time Guide's messages. As you write from your Time Guide's point of view, you may find that your Guide has advice and encouragement for you in all areas of your life, beyond the topic of time.

Also keep in mind that your Time Guide can, like time itself, change and morph according to what you need. For example, you may require something different from your Time Guide at the beginning of a project than you do at the end. Or you may need different types of support in "work time" and in "play time." Specific life events may call for a unique kind of guidance; those intense moments when we "step out of time" are often the moments when we need the most reassurance. When I was a new mom with a newborn, time changed for me so drastically that I was keenly aware of needing a very different kind of support than ever before.

Your Time Guide is a way for you to *always* tune in to the specific frequency of support you need at any given time; you can find the guidance you need in both ordinary and extraordinary times, and discover that those resources are actually already inside you.

ARTsignment: Time Guide

This ARTsignment allows you to identify what you need most from time, calling upon the parts of yourself that need to be heard and compassionately released.

Step 1: Review your responses to the questions in the section "Worrying about Time," earlier in the chapter. Then take some time to answer the following journal questions. I encourage you to write your answers down rather than just thinking about them. The act of writing opens up new portals for discovery and pushes you to be more honest with yourself. Some of the questions may be more applicable to you than others, but I invite you to consider all the questions, even if at first you think they may not be relevant. Take your time, and allow yourself to write "off the beaten path." Feel free to not only write your answers to the questions but write about the feelings you are experiencing, as well.

1. What do you find yourself saying or thinking over and over, about time? (If you're not sure, ask a friend or loved one if there is a recurring theme in what you say about time.)
2. How might your life be different if you did not worry or complain about time?
3. Imagine that you could snap your fingers and all your time anxieties would be gone. Who are you now? What is your first thought and feeling about this prospect?
4. What have you discovered about the roles that worry and anxiety about time play in your life?

Step 2: Close your eyes and allow yourself to relax. Imagine that you could have a Time Guide who would suddenly come to life before you and remain at your side whenever you needed her. What do you need most from this Guide? What kind of guidance, support, advice, or encouragement do you most need, regarding the subject of time?

Step 3: Begin creating a physical form for your Time Guide, using any media or materials you like. As you work, think about your strongest, most powerful wishes and dreams, and allow that positive energy to become infused in every part of the Time Guide's being. Bring more and more life to your Time Guide as you flesh out the details of her personality. Does she have a name? Has she always been a Time Guide? What was she doing before she appeared in your life?

Step 4: When your Time Guide is complete, write a letter to her, asking for her advice. It could start something like this:

Dear Time Guide,
I could really use your help when it comes to Time. I'm feeling…

Here are some more prompts that you could use as you write your letter:

My deepest fear is _____.   I'm really worried about _____.
I really wish _____.   My most powerful dream is _____.
I wish you could tell me _____.   What I need most from you is _____.

Before you close your letter, ask your Time Guide any other questions you may have, or let her know how she can best support you.

Step 5: Situate your Time Guide so that you can look right at her, and read your letter to her, out loud if possible. Read slowly and expressively, so that both you and your Guide can hear the whole range of your feelings. When you've finished reading the letter to your Time Guide, take a new piece of paper or a new page in your journal, and now write a letter *from your Time Guide* to yourself. It could start something like this:

Dear Marney,
I'm so glad you wrote me and shared with me the thoughts in your letter. I want to tell you…

…and continue writing in *her* voice to complete the letter.

As you write, try not to think, plan, or edit the words that come from your Time Guide. Just allow the words to flow through you. If you get stuck, simply allow yourself to write some reassuring words, the kind of words you really want to hear, such as:

It's okay, dear one. You're fine, you're safe, you're beautiful. I'm holding you. We'll get through this together.

Whenever you get stuck, just go back to writing encouraging words, and then allow your pen to keep moving as you unearth what comes next.

ARTsignment Gallery: Time Guide

Digital collage

"My Time Guide is a digital art piece called *Time Tango Muse*. I wanted to capture the ethereal, mysterious nature of time and create a visual illustration of what timelessness feels like. My Time Guide is a tango dancer, the epitome of a helpful partner. She can't dance without me, and I can't dance without her. It takes two to tango; it takes two to design the dance of time." — MARNEY K. MAKRIDAKIS

ARTsignment Gallery: Time Guide

Mixed media assemblage in shadow box, 11 x 8 x 2 in.

"The most significant thing I've discovered through this exercise is that my worrying about time is really just a way to play small and not risk. My Time Guide took the form of the Buddha. He put his arms around me and said in soothing tones, 'It's okay, honey, you have all the time in the world. It's okay to say *no* to things that don't serve you or make you happy. And when you say no, in doing so you will hold a space for the right things to come into your life.' My Guide also had some great ideas to help me remember that I have plenty of time, such as creating a talisman that I can touch anytime to remember that I have all the time in the world for the things that matter most to me."

— VIOLETTE CLARK

ARTsignment Gallery: Time Guide

Mixed media assemblage on dress form, 20 x 7 x 2 in.

"I needed my Time Guide to remind me that life plays out exactly how it is supposed to. I needed to be reminded that I have permission to be happy, to be successful, and to be creative. She told me to *stop* and breathe in the day, and look at the wonder that is all around me right now. She said, 'The future is yours…your destiny is unfolding…you *will* flourish…all you need to do right now is believe in yourself! Permission is yours for the taking!' My Guide has given me permission to let go of my worries about time, to allow them to fly out the window and never knock on my door again!"

— PATRICIA J. MOSCA

ARTsignment Gallery: Time Guide

Mixed media assemblage, 2.5 x 1 x 1 in.

"This is my Precious Time Guide, and she is small enough to sit on my desk or travel in my pocket. She extends time to me as a gift and encourages me to have gratitude for the moment. Her body is made of a key, because her message holds the key to my personal, ever-changing perception of time. Her sparkly, jeweled belly, gold-ribboned arms, and wild curly hair remind me that when I am balanced and aligned, time, light, and energy merge into a creative spirit that takes me on all sorts of wonderful adventures!"

— CHERYL RICHARDS

3. TIME AND RELATIVITY

Poetic Pause

Time as red balloon
Untethered to string theory
Floating beyond us

Einstein's theory of relativity was multifaceted, but at its core it refuted the Newtonian ideas of time and motion, which consisted of the long-held beliefs that motion and time were uniform and absolute. What we generally think of as the theory of relativity actually encompasses two of Einstein's theories: special relativity and general relativity. Einstein introduced his theory of special relativity in 1905, which had several implications for time, including the following:

- Time is relative to the position of the observer who measures it.
- Time is relative to motion.

In 1915, Einstein introduced his theory of general relativity, which expanded on these ideas and offered new implications, such as the effects of altitude and gravitational force on time. In short, Einstein introduced the ideas that motion and time were relative.

Psychological relativity has also been well documented, the term labeling different

Time's Inner Relativity

I asked several colleagues to describe personal experiences with relative perception of time. Here are a few of the responses:

"On a ten-day cruise with my family, time seemed to take on a completely different way of passing during days when we were at sea rather than docking. When things are new and you are engaged in 'experiencing,' time passes quickly. Yet once things have been explored and are then being repeated, time seems to pass ever so slowly. When you are docked and exploring new places, time again flies. The experience was back and forth, like a pendulum."   — Carrie Faden

"When my father was dying from cancer, time seemed to go by so slowly. My mom and I spent about ten months caring for him at home. Now that I look back, ten months was a very short time and it did go by quickly, but at the time the days seemed so slow."
                — Maisen Mosley

"Teaching does strange things to time for me. I tend to watch the time closely, and it goes very slowly; then suddenly I get into it and I'm enjoying the students and the topic, and the time goes so quickly that I end up having to rush to finish what I had planned to do."   — Yvonne Rose

"In college, I was a film student required to take several art classes, and drawing was one of them. I had to spend a weekend working on a huge charcoal drawing of a woman. Spending an entire weekend working on a drawing I knew was terrible was excruciating. It was the longest weekend I ever experienced."   — Bradley Harding

phenomena to define internal relativity of time. For example, the Kappa effect can be seen when considering a journey made in two parts that take an equal amount of time. The journey that covers more distance will appear to take longer than the journey covering less distance, even though they take an equal amount of time. The Tau effect illustrates a similar phenomenon: when we consider a journey made in two parts of equal distance, the part of the journey that takes more time to complete will appear to have covered more distance; thus, a slower journey will appear to cover more ground than a faster one, since it takes more time to complete it.

Aside from fancy psychological terms, we all have had experiences of the *inner relativity* of time…when time seems to move faster or slower, based on our own perception. I have never been more aware of my own inner relativity than in my early days of parenthood, when each day seemed very long, as my sleep-deprived self was lost in a daze of nursing, soothing, and attending to all the needs of a brand-new little human. Yet the weeks and months flew by, as my little baby was already growing and changing all too quickly, and I just wanted time to stop so that I could fully take in every moment. Illness or periods of physical recovery always seem endless when we are in the midst of them, but in retrospect, the time of healing is often quite short in the greater context of a whole life.

In chapter 1, I presented the results of my casual experiment in which fifty-two people created a word collage for what they perceived to be one minute. As the perception varied so greatly, I wanted to see if there were any assumptions or patterns underlying the perceptions reported. After I studied the written comments of the participants, it became clear that they had become more focused on either the *time* aspect of the exercise (trying to make sure that they stopped at one minute) or the *creative* aspect of the exercise (enjoying the process of the word collage). As no particular direction was given either way — participants were told only about what to do and not about where to place their focus — the fifty-two-person sample provided a good mix of experiences. Not unexpectedly, however, those focused on the creative aspect of the exercise were more likely to experience the time as going by faster, and those focused on the time aspect were more likely to perceive the time as moving more slowly. In fact, of those for whom time moved more slowly, 92 percent confirmed that they had been more aware of the clock than of creating.

These examples illustrate how easily our perception of time is altered, simply by the location of our mind's focus. The trouble is that this change in perception is very often the *opposite* of what we want. For example, when we are waiting for something, time moves more slowly, and when we are enjoying something, time moves more quickly. Dan Gremminger summed it up so nicely: "When life is good, the moments cannot last long enough; and when times are not good, they seem to stretch into an eternity." These experiences, when "time works against us," make us feel as if time is controlling us, which results in frustration, confusion, and a loss of existential freedom.

I dislike the popular phrase "a race against time," but it can be useful to explain this point. Imagine that you are moving alongside Time, as two runners in a race — or, for a less competitive analysis, let's think of it as two walkers taking a stroll. We feel content when we are striding alongside Time, in perfect unison. We feel in rhythm, we feel connected, we feel that time is not moving too slowly or quickly. When Time breaks out ahead of us, we feel that it's going too fast and we want it to slow down. When Time lags behind us, we want it to speed up. In either case, our desire is to once again feel the harmonic symmetry that comes when we are one with Time.

RELATIVITY IN ALL THREE STATES OF TIME

Forget-Me-Not

Perhaps ironically, I don't even remember writing this piece, which often happens when I'm in a true creative flow. Even though my memory of creating it seems to be lost in the timeliness of the creative process, I do, however, remember the event that I describe in it, when I sat in a field with my friend Dee Dee, not long before she died. It's a moment alive in my present, so much so that I can hardly even reconcile its placement in the past.

Pocket of Forget-Me-Nots
The mind has these pockets that we unzip from time to time...
You reach in a pocket to recall nine years ago, when you were sitting in a field with a friend, feeling happy to be a bit sad. You remember that feeling, how it bit you casually, and you remember who you were with, the weather, what you were wearing. You remember that you remembered sitting in a similar field as a child. You remember how the ribbons of your hat blew in the breeze, tapping your face with graceful insistence.
You think you've remembered all there is to recall about that moment in the field nine years ago. So you go on about your business. Then, when you least expect it, the pocket unzips a bit more, offering a crystal magnifying glass with which you see even more. And the memory of the way the blue flowers hummed on that day nine years ago comes to saturate your soul.

Internal relativity is present in all three states of time. In the present, our perception is obviously affected by mood and emotion. But past and future time are also affected more strongly by subjective perception than by objective reality. Past time is represented by our memory, yet perhaps nothing is more subjective than individual memory. Who hasn't had the experience of recalling an event with a friend, only to find that the two of you remember completely different things about what happened? Our memories are affected by layers of emotion and judgment, as well as a bizarre combination of change and stasis. In linear time, the past is a straight arrow to the left, but our true experience of past time is multidimensional. We continue to relive and reshape the past as our memories change in color, texture, and even fact. Each time a memory is remembered, it is reshaped, and thus it is relived. We can never remember *all* there is to know about any past event; there is always more to uncover, through the lens of where we are now, as we bring the relative past into the relative present.

Our sense of the future also is affected by our subjective thoughts and feelings about it. "Future time" can feel very far away, or it can feel as close and as real as the present. These vivid connections to future time can be powerful tools. ART-bundance Coach Irina Naskinova realized, "When I can think about things that frighten me and see them from a future point in time, I can see that I have already successfully mastered them. This can give me a lot of confidence to just keep going." Another Coach, Dr. Angela Kowitz Orobko, shared her experience: "When I was in the early stages of my relationship with my husband, I saw myself with him, present with me, even though he was 2,000 miles away at the time. It was an amazing experience. I was profoundly sad when we were apart, but when I vividly visualized myself in the future with him at my side and looking back, that helped me get past those hard moments."

I spend a lot of time envisioning my future work goals very fully and bringing the details to life in the present. When I engage in vision-expanding projects and exercises, the future truly feels just as lively and real as the present. On the other hand, I am aware that in the non-professional areas of my life, the future often feels completely elusive and unknown to me. While I have a very alive and hearty relationship with my professional future, I often tiptoe around the future in my personal life; I don't dare presume or visualize what I want to come to pass, and I can easily fall into the submission of simply living and accepting what is. What a duality! These two very different approaches make me quite aware of the subjective nature of future time.

SARK's Story: The Time Stretcher and Time Shrinker

"When I feel in despair, time seems like the slowest snail ever. When I feel euphoric, it races faster than a comet. If I stay in the 'marvelous messy middle' and do my transformative practices and processes, it feels just about right. I am always experimenting with time on airplanes. Some flights of exactly the same length stretch out like taffy and seem interminable; others seem really quick. So much depends on mood and willingness to suspend time. If I start focusing on 'getting there,' I'm doomed to watch the clock, and everything slows down. If I focus on enjoying exactly where I am, it shifts. I realize that my perception of time is the key; it's not time itself. I created what I call the 'Time Stretcher' and the 'Time Shrinker.' I just call out, 'Time Stretcher, come to me now!' when it appears that there isn't enough time. When I'm doing something I don't like as much, I call on the 'Time Shrinker.' Both of these work really well, and I'm continuing to experiment! I've experimented with this by having fun and joy in the dentist's chair, no matter what they're doing, just by shifting my perceptions of time. I've also experienced an endless summer day of ecstasy by expanding my perceptions of time."
— Susan Ariel Rainbow Kennedy (SARK)

Beyond being such a strong force in all states of time, our relative perception *re-arranges* events into their own sequence and order. Think of two events that feel adjacent to each other in meaning and significance, even though days, weeks, months, or years separate them. An example might be your high school graduation and your child's high school graduation, where the two events feel seamless in your mind. This reordering and resequencing is another example of the way that inner relativity works through time.

RELATIVITY AND TIMEKEEPERS

It's been well documented that clocks themselves are affected by relativity. The Chesapeake Bay experiment proved that clocks run faster at higher altitudes and are affected relative to the earth's rotation. Our experience of clocks is affected by *psychological* relativity, too. Think about how you interact differently with various timekeepers. For example, I interact differently with the clock on the kitchen oven than I do with the clock on my computer, the one at my bedside, or the one in my car. I tend to look at each of these clocks with different anticipations, expectations, and moods. For example, I almost always check the clock in my car to make sure that I'm getting somewhere on time. When I check the clock on my cell phone, it's usually because I'm out and about and I've lost track of the time. The clock in the kitchen is usually related to staying on schedule for my son's mealtime or bedtime.

> "Time is far more complex than I usually assume it to be. My experience of time corresponds to the judgments I'm making about it, so that if I think I don't have enough time, I will be frantic, while if I believe that time is fluid and luxurious, I will relax into its arms."
>
> — JANET SHEPHERD,
> ARTbundance Coach

Of course, our relationship with timekeepers becomes especially relative according to what we are doing. Sometimes we look at a clock with excitement and anticipation (such as when we are waiting for a loved one's plane to land at the airport). Other times we look with stress and anxiety (such as when we're cramming, trying to reach a deadline). Other times still, we look with curiosity (such as when we're spending a leisurely afternoon and have lost track of time, and have no idea what time it is). The same relativity is true with calendars, as our emotions affect the way we turn pages in a datebook or flip the pages in a wall calendar.

Mixed media journal page, 5 x 7 in.

Relative Time by Marilyn Harris Mills

When busy mom Jean E. Sides tried the GratiTimeline ARTsignment in chapter 6, which involves a process of recording gratitude on an hourly basis for one day, she found herself surprised to see that she was looking at her clock with anticipation and excitement as each hour passed. She said, "I set a timer on my cell phone for the hourly notification. I found myself checking my phone before the alarm would go off, eager to record my gratitude. The hours seemed to pass more quickly than normal."

Alarms on clocks have been used for centuries. In the past fifty years, alarm clocks have been used primarily to assist us in awakening at the proper hour. Alarm clocks are the quintessential, albeit often essential, interruption to our natural circadian rhythms. It has only been in very recent years that we have started using alarms for other general purposes besides waking. Now our "smart" gadgets are equipped to offer alarms whenever we like, for appointments, tasks, or anything else that might require a reminder. We can even program them to have different sounds or tones for each type of alarm, again underlining our *relative* relationship to these alarm sounds. My husband and I are in the early stages of designing a new type of alarm that reminds of the preciousness of time and the inherent artistry in the present moment. How wonderful it would be to have an alarm to remind us of the most important appointment of all: attending to this present moment.

RELATIVE PERCEPTION OF TIME

In our daily life, we experience inner relativity most often in the *speed* at which we perceive time to be passing. I asked friends and colleagues to share a personal example of *time seeming to move very fast*, and for an example of *time seeming to move very slowly*. I received many examples, which are summarized in the sidebar "Trends in Temporal Perception."

These examples and this entire chapter explore the fact that the psychological reality of time often means that when we are enjoying ourselves, time moves fast, and when we are nervous, unhappy, or anticipatory, time moves slowly. Does this mean that in order to create more time in our life, we have to be more discontent? Absolutely not. It is helpful to look more deeply at the circumstances that affect the perceived speed of time. In truth, the perception of time is more deeply layered than the platitude "Time flies when you're having fun."

The situations presented in the sidebar represent a wide variety of

Trends in Temporal Perception

Circumstances when time seems to move fast:

- We are doing something we enjoy.
- We are doing a lot of different things at once (be they enjoyable things or not).
- We are engaged in something that comes easily or naturally to us.
- We feel bound in time by the pressure of a deadline.
- Emotional engagement is at a high intensity.
- Positive feelings are present.

Circumstances when time seems to move slowly:

- We are doing something we don't enjoy.
- We are focused on a very specific thing (be it enjoyable or not).
- We are engaged in something challenging.
- We are anticipating or waiting for something.
- Emotional engagement is at a low intensity.
- Positive feelings feel far away.

Pen and ink on vellum with digital color, 6 x 9 in.

there is nothing more I ask, she said, than this moment, exactly so

& she looked at me & my heart danced & forever suddenly seemed too short a time

This Moment, Exactly So by Brian Andreas

circumstances, but notice a simple common denominator: *time moves faster when something else supersedes our inherent attention to time.* In quantum mechanics, it's been proved that the observer has an effect on the observed. A similar effect seems to occur with time: the more we perceive time, the slower it seems to go. The more that something else — whether spending time with loved ones or being in the throes of an unpleasant deadline — overrides our awareness of time, the more quickly it moves.

Knowing this, we can apply some tricks to the very situations where we want to change our perception of the speed of time; you'll see some examples in the discussion of Time Transcendence Tools in the section "Wellativity Step 4," later in this chapter.

THE THEORY OF WELLATIVITY

Since time *is* relative, and is relative on so many levels, why not *consciously* control it, by adjusting our inner relativity? Time is changeable and is not an absolute thing, and we can use this to inspiring advantage. After all, time wasn't even standardized until 1884, and obviously life on the planet was able to carry on just fine before then.

Einstein's theory of relativity is popularly known through the equation $E = mc^2$. In actuality, this equation represents just a portion of the theory of special relativity, basically setting the stage to state that there is equivalence between mass and energy.

I propose a *Theory of Wellativity* that looks like this:

$$F = T + I^2$$

which means:

$$Fulfillment = Time + Imagination^2$$

To summarize the equation: to increase *wellness* in your life, take Time and add to it lots of Imagination, and then you get Fulfillment.

How does imagination play a role in leading us to fulfillment? Imagination is a powerful conduit for change. Applying the dazzling power of imagination is akin to looking through a kaleidoscope. When we look through a kaleidoscope and focus on a single object, the image magically expands into a dazzling infinity of patterns and colors, instantly changing our capacity to see. And when we connect to the power of imagination, sparkly solutions expand in infinite directions, allowing us to

Mixed media on paper, 9.8 x 9.8 in.

Drinking from the Well of Wellativity
by Lanette Breedt

see more. As author and creativity coach Jill Badonsky says, "The imagination is always on call to transport my spirit to that timeless place of inner peace."

The most important changes in my life have, without exception, been primarily fueled by my imagination. Through my imagination, I have attracted an endless number of kaleidoscopic miracles, including bouncing back from mental illness, emerging from suicide attempts, healing physical ailments, attracting my soul mate, designing my ideal work, changing my financial reality, becoming pregnant when doctors said it wasn't possible, losing one hundred pounds, and so much more…including completely changing the way I see and experience *time.*

As my experience, and the examples in the sidebar "Imagination to the Rescue," illustrates, imagination is a *powerful inner creative act*, capable of transforming reality in ways beyond our wildest dreams, including *creating the time we need.* We can use imagination to control our intention, attention, and awareness; by doing so, we can see the ways in which any given period can be shortened or expanded, deepened or cheapened. Through our imagination, we have an infinite capacity to control our perception of time. Knowing that all time is *not* equal opens the doorway for us to tap into imagination to make new choices about how we experience time.

Imagination to the Rescue

Here are some inspiring stories given by people who have used their imagination to help them through challenges:

"One of my favorite visuals is to picture my whole being filled with stars. I once had to go to a gathering of people whom I found very challenging. I wasn't sure how I'd get through the day, and so I pictured laying stars on each person as I talked to them. I had to round up some peace from inside myself, because you can't lay stars on someone when you're feeling negative and rotten."
— Terri St. Cloud

"A time that I used my imagination to help me with a challenge was when a really romantic and infatuated boyfriend cheated on me and broke my heart. I had the idea to go outside and jump-rope each night and pour my heart out as I would cry and jump, connecting with the moon and speaking to her." — Vivian Sakellariou

"When I didn't know how I would get my car repaired, I imagined freedom: what it felt like, what it might look like to have no trouble getting anyplace. As a result, I manifested lots of offers for rides to places I wanted and needed to go, for four months!"
— Melanie Adrienne Hill

"I got together with a girlfriend and we shifted our experience of cleaning house by putting on crazy party hats and throwing ourselves a housecleaning party. We got a whole lot more done than if we had tried to tackle it with a 'woe is me' attitude."
— Jan Blount

In the ARTbundance approach, we say that *any* given topic can be creatively transformed through the following trajectory:

1. Changing our words, thoughts, and feelings about the topic
2. Expanding current awareness of what is
3. Envisioning different ways it could be
4. Actualizing the new vision through action and change

Let's examine each step to see how imagination can be used to transform our experiences with time.

WELLATIVITY STEP 1: CHANGING THOUGHTS ABOUT TIME

The first step uses imagination to control the very words we use and thoughts we think about time. For example, the simple phrase "What time is it?" inherently indicates that we do not have control of our time. By simply replacing this phrase with "What time does the clock say?" we take control of our time through the words we speak. It is a subtle shift, but an important one. The new phrase indicates that we respect the clock, but *we* are the ones creating our time.

In the ARTbundance philosophy, we have a term, *canyon-speak*, that refers to the power of our own words and thoughts and how deftly they are translated back to us in the form of our experience. Canyon-speak describes the metaphor of the universe working like a great big canyon. Whatever we yell into the canyon is echoed back to us in our experience.

If we are saying, "There's never enough time; I'm constantly chasing time and I can't find it," then our experience echoes back, "Yes! There's never enough time; you're constantly chasing time and you can't find it!" If, however, we are saying, "I don't need to find time; I just need to create it. It's all about perception! More and more, I see that I have all the time I need," then your experience is reflected back: "Yes! You don't need to find time; you just need to create it! More and more, you see that you have all the time you need!" What a shift!

Listening to your own canyon-speak about time is a great way to instantly control time's malleability, as Cathleen Spacil discovered: "My biggest challenge as it relates to time is that I always find myself saying, 'There are never enough hours in a day.' So that's what I keep getting: not enough hours in a day! I keep thinking about what Marney says: 'Whatever you yell into the canyon is what you'll hear back.' So now I've tried to catch myself and say I have just the right amount of time, I have plenty of time. It is helping!" After completing some of the ARTsignments in this book, K. Lee Mock expressed, "I became aware that time itself is like a canyon of its own. Don't yell at time and say that it's not there and that it's terrible. Tell time you love it, and it will say it loves you, too."

Digital illustration

$$F = T + I^2$$

FULFILLMENT = TIME + IMAGINATION²

Step 1: Changing our thoughts about time

Step 2: Expanding our awareness of time

Step 3: Envisioning a new kind of time

Step 4: Actualizing the new vision through Time Transcendence Tools

The Steps of Wellativity by Marney K. Makridakis

WELLATIVITY STEP 2: EXPANDING AWARENESS OF TIME

The next step is to use our imagination to *inhabit our current experience of time more fully*. How much of this moment are you fully processing? How much of the past are you remembering and thus integrating into this moment? How fully are you connecting to the future, in the form of visions, dreams, and intentions? The author Diane Ackerman wrote, "I don't want to get to the end of my life and find that I lived just the length of it. I want to have lived the width of it as well." Expanding the width of our moments creates *more* time. When time is wider, we fill it with more *and* take more from it as well.

Here are some suggestions for ways that you can expand time by expanding your awareness of it:

- At any given moment, check in with all of your senses to stimulate an expanded sense of awareness. What do you see, smell, hear, taste, touch, and intuit in this moment right now? Try this at regular intervals throughout the day.

- Catch yourself at moments throughout the day and ask yourself, "How might I experience this moment a little deeper? Feel it a little wider? Accept this moment a little more fully?"

- Gratitude and appreciation are wonderful time expanders. Chapter 6 presents many ideas for incorporating gratitude into your days as a way to transform time.

- Simply remembering to be present expands our awareness. It's amazing how often we are "somewhere else," splitting our focus between moments instead of living in them. Create a mental reminder for yourself, such as tuning in to the present when you walk into a new room, before you check email or answer the phone, or before you eat or drink.

- Focus on the creative potential in each moment. In the traditional culture of Bali, there is no word for "artist," nor a particular label for "creative" people, even though the culture has plenty of artisans, poets, and musicians. In this culture, all activities are equally creative, equally of service. There is no linguistic way to distinguish that a painter's mural is more creative than a farmer's crop. Think about the ways that *you* are being creative in every single moment. Allow yourself to create in everything you do, and feel gratitude for your wonderful creative abilities and all the ways they can be expressed.

- A simple way to experience the *breadth* of time is to use your *breath*. Simply breathing deeply enhances perception and grounds us in the moment.

Perhaps my favorite way to use imagination to expand my current time reality is to mentally "time-travel," extending the current moment in both directions on the timeline, allowing my past and future selves to participate in *this* moment as well. Many quantum physicists have insisted that the past, present, and future exist simultaneously — energetically and even physically. We can use this theory as the basis of imaginative exploration and tap into the energy of these different parts of us that have existed and will exist. A powerful thought experiment is to engage in imaginary time traveling to get more information and insight at any given moment.

To start, ask any question that is strongly on your mind right now. Some examples: "How can I move from living paycheck to paycheck?" "How can I strengthen this relationship?" "How can I make a difference in the world?" Then examine the question *throughout* time, asking yourself at all junctures for information that addresses your question. In other words, answer your question from the point of view of yourself in the womb, as a toddler, as a young child, and so on... all the way to stages older than yourself and at the end of your life. Time's surreal

The Benefits of Time Traveling

Here are some of the responses I got when I presented the "Time Traveling" exercise in a workshop:

"My question was about finding my purpose, and what delighted me and enlightened me at the end was realizing that *loving* is the whole point. I realized that the joy of creativity is a form of loving and sharing, and it has been at all points in my life."

"I asked a question about how to handle clutter, and this exercise reminded me that when I was a child, I loved 'playing house.' I learned that it's time to play house again and have fun as I regain those happy feelings I had making things pretty and orderly as a child."

"I'm in the midst of becoming separated after twenty-nine years of marriage, and this 'time traveling' made me look back and see who I was before I was married, and reminded me about the endless possibilities that await me. This has helped me to have new courage about the path I'm on. My younger selves told me to just go for it, and I was delighted to 'hear' that my older selves did, too."

fluidity can serve a very useful purpose in this exercise, as we find inner knowledge that is available to us only by time-traveling through our own imaginations.

You can even extend your imagination to travel to times long before your birth and long after your death. For example, before Tony and I were married, he wrote a poem for me that depicted our two spirits incarnated as carefree and playful dolphins frolicking in the Atlantic Ocean during the year 1098. When we experience stressful moments in our relationship in present time, I often will time-travel to imagine us as those frolicking dolphins; when I do this, an immediate sense of peace and clarity comes to me. I created the painting shown here to help access and capture these positive feelings, and it hangs in our bedroom.

I especially love "time traveling" to the very end of my life, whenever that may be. I like to imagine that I can ask my wise older self — a luminescent me with white hair

Acrylic on canvas, 24 x 36 in.

Canyons of the Heart
by Marney K. Makridakis

and time-earned wrinkles, a simple question: "What was the best decision you made about such-and-such topic, and why?" Looking at any challenge or choice from her point of view broadens my perspective and never fails to bring me new insight.

To expand our sense of "what is," we can look to another modern scientific hypothesis: the idea of parallel universes. Some scientists believe that there are an infinite number of parallel universes, each the result of cause and effect throughout time. This idea has also taken hold in modern spirituality. The Law of Attraction, for example, is often extrapolated to envision a parallel universe where we already *have* what we want, and therefore we may realize that our desires are *already* manifest.

Parallel universes are extremely helpful in reorienting time to be less about productivity and results, and more about the *process* and *experience*. For example, let's say that I work on a marketing project for three hours and my results produce one hundred sales. I find it helpful to imagine a parallel universe where I got just one sale, as well as a parallel universe where I got one thousand. All three scenarios are equal in terms of time and effort! This exercise helps me realize that the time I put into the work is absolutely the same, no matter what the result. If I have fully inserted myself into the moment, results are not important. This thought helps me expand my sense of what is and, especially, what *is most important*.

WELLATIVITY STEP 3: ENVISIONING A NEW KIND OF TIME

Simply being open to seeing time in a different way is often a great way to start. Try this creative exercise:

1. Write a quick poem by filling in the blanks with the first words that come to mind:

    Time is _____.
    Time is _____.
    Time is _____, _____, and _____.
    Time is _____.
    Time is _____.
    Time is _____, _____, and _____.

2. Next, identify an activity or a state of being during which time seems to stop for you — an activity in which you lose yourself in enjoyment and lose track of time (such as gardening, painting, or meditation).

3. Write a new poem about this activity, following this structure. Fill in the blanks with the first words that come to mind:

(Activity) is _____.
(Activity) is _____.
(Activity) is _____, _____, and _____.
(Activity) is _____.
(Activity) is _____.
(Activity) is _____, _____, and _____.

4. Here's the fun part: In the second poem, every place you wrote your "activity," cross it out and replace it with the word *Time*. Now reread the poem after making the switch. What new ideas and possibilities about time emerge?

In ARTbundance, we call this the Poem Switch, which is an Archeology ARTsignment: a quick creativity exercise that is useful in digging deeper to get to the heart of the matter very quickly. This tool is useful because it is a swift way to grasp what is (that is, what are your current, raw thoughts about time?) and then very quickly transition to what could be (that is, what happens when your thoughts about time are replaced with your thoughts about timelessness?). As Angela Kowitz Orobko said after she completed the exercise, "There was a big shift for me. In the first poem, time was restrictive and negative. In doing the switch, I can see the potential for time to be more uplifting and playful. This feels very hopeful and expansive."

The following are two examples from the Poem Switch Archeology ARTsignment.

Here is Caitlin Anderson's initial poem:

Time is fleeting.
Time is fascinating.
Time is valuable, valued, yet vanishes before my eyes.
Time is limited.

Time is a precious resource.
Time is a resource, takes energy, and is out of my grasp.

Here is Caitlin's rewrite, in which she substituted *Time* for *Swimming*:

Time is peaceful.
Time is happy.
Time is gliding, breathing, and stretching out to my fullest.
Time is the only thing that doesn't hurt.
Time is quiet.
Time is where I do my best thinking, where I swallow water now and then,
     and where I have moments to myself.

Caitlin's response to the exercise: "I have multiple sclerosis, and I need a lot of rest and sleep, and so I'm often feeling like I am 'losing time' because I'd rather be doing other things but my body needs rest. I really appreciate this "poem switch"! I like the notion of time gliding and breathing, as these are things we do without thinking. The second poem shows me a point of view where time feels happy and endless and allows me to stretch out to my fullest."

Unlike in the previous example, Jan Blount's initial poem contained mostly positive, uplifting imagery. And yet she, too, experienced a shift in doing the rewrite. Here is Jan's initial poem:

time is flowing
time is moving
time is aging, wrinkled, cyclical
time is a spiral
time is a line
time is a dot, exclamation point, question mark

Here is Jan's rewrite, in which she substituted *time* for *dancing*:

time is joy
time is sensual
time is rhythmic

time is wild, fun, connecting
time is leaps
time is spins and grace
time is story, play, a hug

Jan's response to the exercise: "While there is some movement expressed in my first version, I notice that overall my first version conveys time as more static. My second version conveys more intensity, energy, and movement. I also notice that the first version feels more serious and heavy in tone, and the second one has a lighter, playful feeling that I really like."

The Poem Switch Archeology ARTsignment is a great preparation for the rest of the activities in the book, and I encourage you to try it yourself. By simply using your imagination to see that time *could be* different, you open yourself to welcoming in a new reality.

WELLATIVITY STEP 4:
ACTUALIZING NEW TIME WITH TIME TRANSCENDENCE TOOLS

The final progression is to use imagination to *actualize* a new view of time. Our actions provide the legs for change; imagination provides the precious momentum behind the action.

One way to actualize a new sense of time is to *consciously control time's relative speed*. Earlier in this chapter, I proposed that our perception of time is directly related to our awareness of it. Whenever any element can override our awareness of time, time moves more quickly. We can use this knowledge to our advantage to slow and quicken time according to our desire. For example, when do you want time to slow down? You might want to *consciously slow down* time when you are enjoying yourself, when you're engaged in a meaningful moment that you don't want to end, when you are running late, or when you need more time to make a decision or accomplish a task or goal.

On the other hand, when do you wish time would speed up? You might want to *consciously speed up* time when you are engaged in something you dislike, when you're in pain, when you're doing something tedious, when you're waiting in anticipation for something exciting to happen, or when you're working toward a goal that seems to be taking a long time.

Try activating these Time Transcendence Tools: ways to consciously slow down or speed up your perception of time.

Time Transcendence Tools: Slowing Time

1. **Create focused time rather than scattered time.** Multitasking severely alters our sense of time by speeding it up. When I am feeling stretched for time while working, my very best tool is to turn off the phone, disable email and the Internet, and simply focus on one thing. It's amazing how time seems to slow down when I have reduced distractions to a minimum.

2. **Focus on segmentation rather than wholeness.** The more segmented time is, the slower it seems to go; the passing of days seems collectively slower than the passing of years. So when you want to slow time, rather than thinking "I have only two hours to spend with my loved one," focus on the fact that you have 120 precious minutes, or 7,200 seconds, to fill. That's a lot of time!

3. **Create a Time Wrap.** When it feels as if life is moving so fast that you might be in a time warp, you can create a Time Wrap: a mental image of a moment wrapped up and safely cocooned in time. Simply imagine that you are wrapping yourself in the moment, protected from outside pressures. When I first made the decision to focus solely on family on the weekends, I created the transition from workdays to weekends with a short visualization of my family in a little bubble, where I could not be distracted by any worries away from the moment. I still start off each weekend by "putting us in the bubble," a sacred Time Wrap of protective bliss.

4. **Slow down.** When you are trying to finish a task and you're running out of time, the inclination is to move very quickly. But by moving slowly, deliberately, intentionally, you actually slow your own perception of time, to give yourself more mental time and creative space to complete your project.

5. **Place yourself in circular time.** Imagine yourself moving at the same speed as the earth's rotation. The spinning of the earth on its axis is a

splendid example of circular time, time that continues circuitously and renews itself. To slow down time and regain a sense of balance, mentally align yourself with moving at the speed of the earth, centered on your own axis of gravity.

6. **Connect with your senses.** Several people related that during crises, time seems to slow down; in the process, they become more aware of their senses. When we want time to move slowly in noncrisis situations, we can re-create this sensation of slowing time by connecting with our senses. Imagine that all of your senses have a volume switch that you can turn up, to tune in to sight, smell, taste, touch, and intuition more deeply. This is a very effective way to slow time.

7. **Notice *everything* happening.** We can slow time down by noticing everything that is happening at once, right now. Notice all the colors, motions, sounds, smells, and feelings that you can observe right in your immediate setting. Then expand your thoughts to think about *everything that is happening* right now in this moment. At this very moment, think about how many babies are being born, how many new businesses are starting, how many people are weeding the garden. Simply sitting with this sensation of perpetual motion places our focus on time, and thus expands it.

8. **Take mental snapshots.** Photography is a useful metaphor for slowing down time. By default, our brains seem to work like some kind of quantum video camera, seamlessly recording the moments as they pass. Instead, imagine that your mind is a still camera, manually clicking a photo of each moment. Just as a photographer can alter the speed at which his camera shoots, you too can slow down your mind's camera to capture the moment at any speed you like. Later, you can "develop" your mental photographs by reflecting on them, again, at your choice of speed, just as a photographer selects the speed of exposure in the darkroom. In both cases, the choice of speed is yours; you control it simply with your awareness.

9. **Engage in activities of high time awareness.** Consciously engaging in activities that are naturally soaked through and through with temporal significance slows down time without our even realizing it. Engage in

games or activities based on timing, such as timed creative challenges like the word collage presented in the first chapter. Time yourself as you do your daily activities and plot them on a chart. Whenever you have the feeling that you just want the whole world to slow down, try spending time with babies and the elderly; this connects you to a keen awareness of the life cycle and an understanding that your perception of "life zipping by" is just that: your perception alone.

10. **Tithe your time.** The ancient tradition of tithing typically refers to giving one-tenth of your income to charity. Religious traditions see tithing as a way to practice faith; spiritual traditions see tithing as a way to welcome more abundance. I believe that the universe automatically circulates the flow of money all the time, and tithing allows us to *consciously direct* where we want the outgoing flow to go. It is the same with time. By viewing your time as a resource, you can tithe 10 percent of your time to a cause that matters to you. The less time you feel you have to donate, the greater the potential these types of activities have to expand your vision of time.

Time Transcendence Tools: Speeding Up Time

1. **Create scattered time rather than focused time.** Variety and diverse foci speed time up. So when you want time to move faster, increase your points of focus. Multitasking is a great way to accomplish this. But even if you are working on a task that requires sole focus, you can still accomplish the same thing by scattering your mental focus. When I am doing a mundane administrative task, my best way to get through it and make the time go by faster is to turn it into a game: vary the patterns, give myself points, add more rules to the game to change it up. Rapidly changing our point of focus, whether internally or externally, also increases the *rapidity of time.*

2. **Focus on wholeness rather than segmentation.** Since segmenting time seems to slow it down, when you want time to speed up, focus on larger units of time measurement. For example, you can think about an entire unbearable hour in the dental chair, or you can think of it as a silly,

incredibly tiny and downright inconsequentially small fraction (1/8,760) of a year!

3. **Connect to your passion.** When something takes us away from our awareness of time, this speeds up our perception of its passing. Nothing is better at distracting us from temporal awareness than engaging in our passions; this is why we lose track of time when we are doing things we love. So, use this virtually universal truth in your favor: in the moments when you want time to go faster, simply find a way to engage with your passion. For example, my friend Bradley Harding often finds a way to connect to filmmaking when he is in unpleasant situations. He shares, "During Catholic church services as a youth, I would write epic horror films in my head. Today, I use my passion as a writer and filmmaker to sometimes change the way I perceive time, and I often fall back on my churchgoing experiences when I am enduring something I would rather not, and create a potential story or character idea in my head."

4. **Look for lessons.** When time is moving slowly, there is often a reason for its slowing pace. My genetic bone disorder has led to numerous injuries and surgeries, and many extended periods when I've had limited physical mobility. Months on crutches can feel like a lifetime, and on  the surface, I'm always wanting those times to move faster. However, I cannot deny that the times when I have been physically limited have always, without fail, seemed to unlock *other* kinds of motion and movement. For example, when I was in a rehab hospital after a knee replacement at age thirty-one, time crawled much more unbearably slowly than it ever had before, and yet that is also when I came up with the idea for Artella and the vision to follow it through. Last year I broke my foot, and it took multiple surgeries and the entire year to heal. This was very frustrating, as it dramatically limited my activities. Yet, during that time, I developed wonderful new self-care practices, since I wasn't able to exercise. While these awarenesses may not directly speed up time, in both examples they helped me to stop fighting against time's trajectory, so that I no longer felt I was "running behind." As long as we're *learning*, time is probably moving at just the right speed.

5. **Engage in physical movement.** As my story above illustrates, time definitely seems to slow down when our motion is constricted. So, to speed up time, we can move our bodies more. When you're working at a mundane task at the computer, put on some dance music and let your body groove to make the task go more quickly. When cleaning the house, add more physical movement than may be necessary for a given task. In a wonderful serendipity of joy and efficiency, connecting with motion and rhythm truly does change the motion and rhythm of time.

6. **Engage in mental movement.** I've found that I can shrink time simply by activating a sense of movement in my imagination. For example, look at a painting and imagine it coming to life, much as the Toulouse-Lautrec painting comes alive in the film *An American in Paris*. Or imagine a potter's wheel and the endless motion of creativity it generates. Exercises like these are wonderful ways to experiment with the malleability of the moment, and if you allow yourself to get lost in these visualizations, you'll be surprised at how quickly time has passed.

7. **Fill yourself up.** An inspiring woman named Irina Naskinova, the head Web programmer on Artella's team and an ARTbundance Coach, offered these words that truly touched me: "Surprisingly, I found that if I manage to love the ragged parts of myself, I get full, and completing my tasks comes easily. Isn't it strange how things unrelated to time help?" Taking care of yourself and nurturing yourself deeply is a wonderful way to remove both conscious and subconscious attachments to time, which frees you up immensely.

8. **Pass the remote.** When time is moving slowly, just imagine that you have a remote control and can fast-forward to a time when whatever you are anticipating is done. One woman used this technique with regard to the presentation she made: "I have a deep fear of public speaking, and so I imagined the time when the date of the presentation was behind me, and I was finished with it. I could see that I was able to survive it and it had enriched me with lessons."

9. **Connect with others.** Spending time with enjoyable people naturally speeds up time, so we can use this to our advantage during those moments when we wish time would move just a bit faster. Call a friend at regular intervals, even if for only a minute or two, when you're cleaning

the house. Instant-message a buddy when you're working on an arduous computer task. Invite a friend over for a visit when you're waiting for important news. When we are in any state of anticipation, we can often feel a bit hollow and unformed, which leads to a dragging sense of time. Through the power of *connection*, we can connect the dots, filling the empty spaces of our psyche.

10. **Time-lapse yourself.** Time-lapse photography is a cinematography technique in which the frequency of the frames being recorded (referred to as the *frame rate*) is much lower than the rate used to play the sequence back. When the sequence is replayed at normal speed, time appears to be moving faster. Slow processes, such as seasons changing or fruit rotting, are time-lapsed in their quick, seamless playback. When you want time to move more swiftly, imagine that the moment you are in is being played back at the quickened pace of a time-lapsed scene in a film. To align yourself with this quickened pace, you might want to search for "time-lapse photography videos" online and feel your own inner pace quickening as you watch them. There is even a popular iPhone app that allows you to time-lapse your day through photographs!

ARTSIGNMENT: WELLATIVITY ART

This ARTsignment allows you to further reflect on the power of imagination to control your experience of time, as you illustrate the Theory of Wellativity in a personal, meaningful way.

Step 1: Create a piece of artwork to illustrate the following equation, introduced in the section "The Theory of Wellativity," earlier in this chapter:

$$F = T + I^2$$

(Which means, as you might recall, Fulfillment = Time + Imagination^2). Create the art to depict what this equation means to you and what it stands for.

Step 2: As you create, decorate and embellish the artwork with images and words representing the concepts and ideas from this chapter that you most want to remember. In other words, create the artwork to be a tangible takeaway not only to remind you of the equation itself, and your thoughts and feelings about it, but also to remind you of the specific ideas and suggestions given that feel most valuable to you.

ARTsignment Gallery: Wellativity Art

Mixed media on paper, 8.5 x 11 in.

Front

Sample views when opened

"At first I felt challenged in how to adequately create a piece of art that reflects the constant motion of time. I happily found a way to represent time's fluidity, how it contracts and expands according to my perception. Like time, this art piece is engineered to be interactive, reminding me to be aware of time's ever-unfolding possibilities as I twist and turn it, flipping it to open again and again, revealing lessons, reminders, and affirmations. My greatest takeaway is that my perspective affects all of my life experience, and by shifting my perspective, I can transcend time. When I intentionally shift my perspective, I create my reality and my experience of now."

— KELLY NOEL MORRISON

ARTSIGNMENT GALLERY: WELLATIVITY ART

Chalk and graphite pencil on paper, 16.5 x 11.7 in.

"Time transcendence was a delicious theme to peruse. I drew a dandelion in seed form, floating in the breeze, symbolizing perfection in the moment as it drifts to find a new home to grow and bloom in the support of loving connected energies. To me, the Wellativity equation reminds me of my own embryonic image: myself contained in a loving cocoon as time is wrapping me up and nurturing me while I 'let go and let God.'" — CALLIE CARLING

ARTsignment Gallery: Wellativity Art

Collage with digital enhancement

"Creating this collage led to new portals of understanding about how time works in my life. As I selected the words and images that spoke to me, I felt as if I were on a leisurely train ride that suddenly transitioned to warp speed and then slowed again, allowing me to see a slice of time as the *whole* of human experience. There are infinite possibilities in a single moment, and there is a flowing, emerging *whole* from what, at first glance, seem to be mere fragments of broken time. Time, it seems, is on my side and pulsing through me as I am through it."   — DAWN RICHERSON

4. KRONOS AND KAIROS

Poetic Pause

Time as laughing gods
To think, we might understand?
Sitcom in the sky

There is an interesting historical context for a subjective perception of time that can help prepare the way for the conceptual journey of creating time. The ancient Greeks had two words for marking the differences between the experiences of time: *kronos* and *kairos*. My father, Lonnie Kliever, a university professor in the philosophy of religion, wrote an article about kronos and kairos for the very first issue of my then-brand-new *Artella* magazine, back in 2003. His description of the concepts kronos and kairos is still the best way I know to explain it:

> *As usual, the Greeks were ahead of us in thinking and speaking about such conundrums. Where we use one word to describe a whole range of things, they had the good sense to use different words to mark distinctions in reality and in experience. For example, they had three different words for the experience of love — eros for possessive love, philia for friendly love, and agape for sacrificial love. Not surprisingly, the Greeks had two words for marking the differences between the experiences of time — kronos and kairos.*

Kronos (or cronos *in the English spelling, from which we take our word* chronology) *is sequential time. Kronos is the time of clocks and calendars; it can be quantified and measured. Kronos is linear, moving inexorably out of the determinate past toward the determined future, and has no freedom. Kairos is numinous time. Kairos is a time of festivals and fantasies; it cannot be controlled or possessed. Kairos is circular, dancing back and forth, here and there, without beginning or ending, and knows no boundaries.*

Like most mysteries of nature and life in the ancient world, these different experiences of time were seen as the manifestations of different gods. The Greeks represented time with nine different gods, but the main gods of time were Kronos and Kairos. Kronos, the god of the world and time, was the most important of the Elder Gods. He was Lord of the Universe, the source of life and death. He devoured his own children to prevent them from replacing him as the supreme god, but his wife saved their last son, Zeus, who eventually overthrew his father's relentless rule of life and death.

By contrast, Kairos was one of the subtlest gods in the Greek pantheon. He was portrayed as a winged god, dancing on a razor's edge. In one hand he held the scales of fate. He reached

Where Kronos and Kairos Kiss

My first memory of these two Greek words for time is from my wedding day in 2000. A longtime family friend who officiated the ceremony, Bill O'Brien, referenced the terms during the ceremony, which was an apt touch, since my husband-to-be was Greek. In welcoming our friends and loved ones, Bill said, "This moment is a time *between* the times. A time *without* a time. A sacred moment, a holy moment, carved out by love's integrity. A moment...*where kronos and kairos kiss.*"

Kronos and kairos smooched again on an auspicious day a decade later. On the day when Tony and I celebrated our tenth wedding anniversary, we discovered that a video of our wedding ceremony existed, and we hadn't even known it! The discovery of this treasure was so powerful, it made me realize the importance of creating time capsules to uncover at surprising moments. As Tony and I watched this uncovered treasure-on-tape, we celebrated ten years of marriage in kronos time and were able to relive our wedding through the serendipity of kairos time. We were once again wrapped in a moment where kronos and kairos kiss, getting our own little glimpse of eternity in a tandem embrace.

out with the other hand to tip those scales, altering the course of fate. Kairos was the god of lucky chance. He personified numinous moments of time giving birth to novelty and surprise.

Drawing on these ancient mythic images, we can revisit the two kinds of time with deeper understanding. Kronos is mechanistic and deterministic, time that is ruled by the dead hand of the past. Kronos devours us with remorseless certainty. Kronos turns life into stone. Kairos is creative and serendipitous. Kairos is time that is energized by the living dream of the future and presents us with unlimited possibility. Kairos turns fate into destiny.

We are not helpless to tip the balance in the direction of kairos over kronos. We can temper our fear and our fixation on sequential time. We can deepen our quest and our experiences of numinous time. In such synchronicity of kronos and kairos lies our deepest consolation and our steepest aspiration.

Digital collage

Cascading Kairos by Marney K. Makridakis

My father passed away several years ago, but these words are a bittersweet reminder that timeless wisdom often extends beyond a chronological life's last breath. By embracing the idea of kairos, we move beyond chronology and begin to view our time and our entire life in nonlinear, expansive terms, opening up to rich opportunities for inspiration. Through this simple change in perspective, we begin to see how we too can travel through time, and how we can even connect to eternity, as our words, art, and actions of today can reverberate throughout the universe forever, just as my dad's words are echoing here in this chapter.

KRONOS AND KAIROS IN EVERYDAY LIFE

Kairos and Goals

Many people are overwhelmed by the linear nature of the goal-achievement process. It is easy to get lost in the expected "order" of the goal process by obsessing over what needs to be done first or feeling like we can't take action until something *else* happens first. When I work with creative professionals on their entrepreneurial goals, I often invite them to envision the trajectory of their goal in kairos time. Think of a goal in your own mind right now, and imagine that this goal could be suspended in linear time. What might it mean if you suddenly were allowed to do things *out of order*, or do things in the "wrong" sequence, because linear time did not exist?

Momentum and motivation are generated by *movement*, not sequential modularity. *Any* movement releases productivity. As Thoreau said, "If you have built castles in the air, your work need not be lost; that is where they should be. Now put the foundations under them." Kairos allows us to glimpse the grace of possibilities that exist outside of expected order.

I have found the distinction between kronos and kairos to be very helpful in normal, everyday circumstances. By consciously inserting myself into one or the other, I can influence the way I experience time. During my workday, if I'm having a hard time moving from a fun, creative task into a deadline-driven administrative one, simply being aware of the fact that I'm moving from kairos to kronos can ease the transition. The distinction also helps me to better understand my own reactions when I get frustrated about time. For example, when I'm feeling frustrated that my young son is moving too slowly while we're getting ready to go somewhere, I can realize, "Okay, I'm just feeling frustrated because I'm in kronos right now. Do I really need to be?" With this realization, I can let myself off the hook for perhaps being a little too rigid, and then lighten up a bit; maybe pretending

Mixed media on canvas, 18 x 18 in.

Time in My Image by Marilyn Harris Mills

that Kai's socks are wild tickle puppets is, after all, more important than getting there "on time."

I have learned so much about kairos from watching Kai and the way he perceives time. Kai was born in Hawaii, and his name comes from the Hawaiian word for "ocean." The connection between his name and the Greek word for spiritual time is just a happy coincidence, but as you'll explore in chapter 12, such synchronicities are moments that bump up against one another in time and often hint at deep experiences *that take us out of time and insert us back into it.* These days, little Kai is indeed my kairos, in the way he embodies not just timelessness but time-fullness.

> "*Kairos, to me, is where the opening of all possibility and pure potential meets the immediate need of the individual, causing the manifestation of exactly what we need at the exact moment that we need it found in absolute expansiveness.*"
>
> — CARRIE FADEN,
> ARTbundance Coach

Due to the genetic metabolic bone disorder he inherited from me, Kai has already been through a lot of medical challenges in his brief life. He has done a lot of living in a little time, making the number of

Digital collage

My Kairos by William J. Charlebois

years in his quantifiable lifetime up to now seem rather irrelevant. Kai is much smaller in stature than most kids his age but has a giant personality; like kairos, he cannot be defined by any linear measurement. Kai is always fully engaged in the present moment and also easily flits away to something new that catches his fancy, like a butterfly seeking nectar. When I tell him, "It's one o'clock, time to go to nap," he is likely to say something like, "Okay, but I have another plan: let's play!" Kai, like all toddlers, lives in kairos and creates his own time.

It is up to each of us to define our own kairos and to create kairos in our own image. Kairos, as the embodiment of creative, numinous, spiritual time, reminds us that we can move out of kronos at will, to create our own time.

ARTSIGNMENT: CREATE YOUR KAIROS

This ARTsignment guides you to discover what you want *your* kairos to be. We may not always be able to live in our ideal kairos, but our ideal kairos can in fact always live within us; the opportunity to create your own kairos fully welcomes this joyous reality!

Step 1: Answer the following journal questions to further investigate your ideal concept of kairos time.

1. Kairos represents numinous time. The dictionary definitions of *numinous* include "supernatural, spiritual, mysterious, holy, filled with the sense of the presence of divinity, appealing to the higher emotions or to the aesthetic sense." What does *numinous time* mean to you? How might you experience numinous time in your life?

2. Kairos represents circular, dancing time, without beginning or end. What does *circular time* mean to you? How might you experience circular time in your life?

3. Kairos is the god of lucky chance. What does *lucky chance time* mean to you? How might you experience lucky chance time in your life?

4. Kairos is creative, serendipitous, energized by fantasy and the living dream of the future. What does this kind of *fantastical time* mean to you? How might you experience fantastical time in your life?

5. Kairos represents the moments when time gives birth to novelty and surprise. What does this kind of *birthing time* mean to you? How might you experience this kind of surprise-birthing time in your life?

6. What other things would you like your own kairos to represent?

7. Summarize your favorite things that you've written here (and add more, if you'd like) to create a description of what kairos means to you.

8. What does your kairos *look* like? Imagine how you might incorporate symbols of each element of your description into a visual representational figure of your kairos.

Step 2: Take the ideas and symbols you just imagined, and incorporate them into a piece of art that represents a figure of your kairos. As my father explained in his article earlier in the chapter, the ancient Greeks represented kairos as a winged god, dancing on a razor's edge. In one hand he held the scales of fate. He reached out with the other hand to tip those scales, altering the course of fate. What symbolism would you like to incorporate into your image of kairos?

Step 3: As you work, think about what your life would be like if you could live in kairos time, as you have defined it. Enjoy dreaming, imagining, fantasizing, as you dance with new ideas of time.

Step 4: After you have completed your kairos, reflect on the relationship between kronos (traditional, sequential time) and kairos (your own interpretation of nonsequential time) in your own life. How might they help each other? How might they work together, then join hands to work with you?

ARTsignment Gallery: Create Your Kairos

Watercolor collage on paper, 18 x 24 in.

"I have often felt overwhelmed by the limits of time, when in reality, time is limitless in itself. My kairos is a series of Möbius strips (infinity symbols). Making them was an experience of complete bliss. I used cool colors; then I felt the need for action in my kairos for the part of time that makes things happen. I introduced radiant reds, oranges, and yellows like the rays of the sun or a star around the Möbius strip. These rays of warm colors give me the sense of movement and action, as the Möbius strip of kairos carries on and on around and around for all eternity."

— DR. ANGELA KOWITZ OROBKO

ARTsignment Gallery: Create Your Kairos

Digital illustration

"My attempt was to personify both kairos and kronos and their relationship. The fairy creature of kairos morphed into an ageless and timeless magical goddess. For kronos, I attempted to visually convey as many time-measuring devices as I could, including a metronome, tree rings, and an egg timer. They are caught in their own lockstep cycle, forever ticking and tocking through the planets and their civilizations. And like a magical breeze, kairos is able to flit through the rigid structure of 'clock' time. The liberating spirit of kairos laughs at our inability but respects our desire to define and control Time."
— DAN GREMMINGER

ARTsignment Gallery: Create Your Kairos

Stone altar (partial view), 8 x 8.5 x 9 in.

"I came to see that working and trusting my intuition (lucky chance time) is an important tool for me to actively use. After doing the journal questions, I attended a retreat and collected rocks from the dried-out riverbed. I envisioned building an altar with them. I then understood *why* I was doing this ARTsignment: these rocks are my kairos. The symbolism is elemental: earth, water flow, holes in which the air moves through. I love that change can be made by simply moving the stones to new positions when sitting with them. They are altered as kairos calls to be."

— VIVIAN SAKELLARIOU

ARTsignment Gallery: Create Your Kairos

Mixed media assemblage on board, 24 x 12 in.

"This piece represents my kairos and the miracles kairos time has granted through-out my life. This piece is a reminder to me that the Divine is supporting me and my dreams, and to trust in that Higher Power. It's a reminder that there is never lack of time. Time is infinite and plentiful. My kairos creation highlights things I have made time for in my life, things I wish I'd made more time for in my life, and things I still hope and plan to make time for in my life. This whole project has been a great reminder that time is infinite, and that even the smallest amount of time can be used productively. Not surprisingly, little miracles of 'found time' and synchronici-ties helped me to create this project along the way."
— WENDY FEDAN

SECTION 2

CREATING TIME
THROUGH CREATIVITY

5. Creating Time through Flow

Time Sighs When You're Having Fun

Poetic Pause

Time as a comma
Pausing between nothingness
Curved like a question

The perception of time is the quintessential human paradox. We often want to escape ourselves and lose track of time, and yet when we become fully aware of the gift of time, we are more present and in touch. As mentioned in chapter 1, I see a solution in *becoming less aware of time but more aware of the present moment*. This leads us to a certain state of bliss that often is described as "losing track of time" or "timelessness."

We all have had moments when we lost track of time or became unaware of the time passing. There are several ways to describe such experiences. In 1964, Abraham Maslow coined the term *peak experiences* to explain those moments when we are fully engaged with something outside ourselves. In his book *Finding Flow: The Psychology of Engagement with Everyday Life*, Mihaly Csikszentmihalyi popularized the concept of *flow*, a mental state in which we are fully immersed in what we are doing through energized focus, full involvement, and success in the process of the activity.

During peak experiences or flow activities, it's not so much that time goes faster, but that time seems to dissolve altogether. We've all heard that time flies when we are having fun, but when I've been in the flow state, I have felt that time neither flies nor stalls…instead, time *sighs*. When we have those experiences of time sighing, everything feels different. The example that sticks out for me occurred several years ago, when we had just moved to Hawaii and my husband had returned to the mainland to finish packing up our home there. I spent two months in a new home, on an island where I didn't know anyone. It was a unique opportunity for inward exploration and reflection, and it triggered the most prolific period of creativity I'd ever experienced. With few responsibilities or obligations, and with no sense of linear time, I did little else but paint wildly colorful canvases around the clock.

Acrylic on canvas, 18 x 24 in.

I Paint the World, the World Paints Me
by Marney K. Makridakis

I can remember a sensation of blurriness in the air as I was painting, as if the edges of my experience were fusing into something else, perhaps the very borders of time fading away. Though I've never felt it again to quite that extent, I still recognize this gossamer-silk sensation during times when I am in a creative flow; I've even experienced it a few times as I've been writing this book. I don't know what it means, and I can scarcely even describe it; I just know that everything takes on a different quality when we are in the flow, when time is sighing. When I asked students to describe their experience during the flow state, they shared some of the following impressions:

- "Colors become brighter."
- "I feel a buzzing sensation inside."
- "I feel really, really awake."
- "There's a bit of sparkle in the air."

As a child, I remember, I fantasized about what it would be like to live inside of a snow globe. I think this fantasy was rooted in growing up in Texas and longing for snow. And yet, even then, perhaps part of me longed for the still perfection of a glitter-filled utopia and the metaphor for time-lessness that it provides. In those sparkly little dome-shaped wonderlands, there is only the present, only the now, only *that* world. Nothing else matters — appointments, responsibilities, negotiations. Everything is flowing, shimmer-ingly encapsulated in the moment, encased in a *flow* globe.

> *"Doing what I love automatically causes the flow of creativity, and helps me feel more like myself."*
>
> — JANET LAIRD,
> ARTbundance Coach

In real life, we can call it *flow, peak experi-ence,* or *losing track of time* — different labels to describe the same type of experi-ence, an experience that we all seem to crave. These timeless moments align us with the truisms of who we are. They unify us with the world on which we spin. And they provide our souls with deep evidence that outside of the obvious mortal limitations we have on this planet, the perception of time is completely subjective, and just as it was when we were children, time is therefore always under *our* control instead of the other way around.

TIMELESSNESS AND AUTHENTICITY

We approach timelessness in the moments when we feel most at home with our-selves. When we are being true to ourselves and existing in authenticity, we are not measuring ourselves against time or anything else. We are simply *being*, and this opens a doorway to flow.

My son, Kai, deals with a lot of physical pain from his medical issues, so it's always quite easy to tell when he's "not himself." As a toddler, he has not yet learned to edit himself or pretend to be something he's not. On a recent day when he was having one of these not-himself afternoons, it occurred to me that it's often more difficult to identify when we, as grown-ups, "aren't ourselves." Ironically, our own authenticity can be challenging to grasp. Perhaps it's because we have so many "selves" that we don't know which one is really us. Martin Luther King wrote, "Each of us is something of a schizophrenic personality, tragically divided against ourselves," and I think that modern society certainly perpetuates this division. Or maybe it's because we're so used to just "getting by" in our day-to-day routines that we forget it's even possible to remember who we really are.

If you can relate to this odd paradox, I invite you to try a simple exercise and see if it makes a difference. Stop throughout the day and ask yourself, "How much do I feel like me...the real, true me?" I've found this simple question to be so helpful in getting in touch with the essence of when I am happiest, most productive, and most centered.

A good place to start is to think about your life, pinpointing the times when you have felt most whole and the most comfortable in your skin. Using those moments as touch points, look at your current life; and for the next several days, check in with yourself often to become aware of when you are feeling more, or less, authentic to your true self. Sometimes questions arise when you aren't sure if you are really being you at any given time or if you are trying to be the you that you strive to be. Generally speaking, as long as the intended you is coming from an authentic place in the current you, then you are on the right track.

Acrylic on board, 7 x 7 in.

Go with Your Flow by Patricia J. Mosca

One particularly helpful technique is to plot points on an informal graph that you can quickly sketch as you go about your routine. Ask yourself throughout the day if something feels right to you and feels true to you, and mark it on a graph, chart, or map. This practice creates an authenticity meter of sorts and allows you to start recognizing patterns in your life.

Be gentle with yourself in your explorations, and view your insights with curiosity rather than judgment. As we all know, development and growth have their awkward, even clumsy stages; this is applicable not only for physical growth but also as we settle into our constantly evolving emotional, spiritual, and mental "skins." Sometimes inner growth is smooth and easy, as many books and gurus make it out to be, but often it just happens one little halting step at a time. In spite of our awkward fumblings, day-to-day life doesn't have to be drudgery. When we connect with flowing authenticity, life can be a dance — a dance with the most daring and exciting partner of all, your true self.

WHAT GETS US IN THE FLOW?

When we get lost in time, there is actually no loss at all; as parts of us are *found*, it becomes an expansive experience. Circumstances that trigger a flow state are different for everyone, but several common circumstances tend to promote this state. For example, flow often happens for me when I step away from my normal environment. When we are in new settings, we are separated from the usual context of our routine, and so we temporarily are displaced from time. For this reason, much of this book was written in different places: on note cards at the lake, on a laptop in cafés. Even in my own home, I find it helpful to move away from my desk and write on the living room couch or on the playroom floor. For me, flow seems to be attracted to new locations.

New environments and circumstances might inspire a flow state, but flow doesn't require expensive supplies or fancy settings. Nor does flow require a lot of time. My friend Jill Badonsky, an author and creativity coach, wisely advises, "One of our biggest blocks is thinking we need to spend a 'block' of time on our creativity. Show up small and notice that you sink into a spell of timelessness and your Muse won't let you leave." I wholeheartedly agree; flow doesn't seem to know or care if we

Go with the Flow

Go with the Flow

Flow happens when we are:

- Engaged
- Introspective
- Aware
- Connected
- Invigorated
- Positively challenged
- Curious
- Involved
- Comfortable
- Giving or serving
- Connecting to ourselves
- Connecting with others
- Feeling the meaning in what we are doing

have five minutes or five hours to lose ourselves. It's *our* judgments about lack of time that get in the way.

Of all the things that get us in the flow — many of which are listed in the sidebar "Go with the Flow" — the element of *meaning* is perhaps the most important. Creativity, meaning, and time dance together in an unavoidable, and rather effective, cycle: the more meaningful your projects are to you, the more likely you are to engage in them. Then, the more meaning you are experiencing, the more creative ideas you'll have for more meaningful projects. Meaning creates more meaning, and creativity begets creativity!

And, of course, regularly making the *time* for meaningful acts cements their importance in your life.

FINDING FLOW IN EVERYDAY LIFE

Once we identify the things that get us in a flow state, not only can we take steps to engage in them more often, but also we can work on inserting the essence of those things whenever we are doing other, seemingly nonflow activities. If you lose track of time when making art, think about how to integrate more art into your daily life. Can you add doodles on the envelopes when you pay your bills or write haikus in your head while you do the dishes? If spending time in nature gets you in the flow state, perhaps you could leave your office to take your lunch break in the outdoors or volunteer in a community garden.

Finding flow in everyday life is all about discovering ways to fill more and more of your time with the things that matter most to you, the things that fill you with curiosity, joy, wonder, and awe. As your life becomes more filled with meaning, inevitably you find that time as a theme in your life matters less and less and the richness of each present moment matters more and more.

Another way to find flow in daily life is to bring a sense of *flowing time* into *all* time. One way to do this is to align yourself with a *circular* rather than a linear sense of time. Simply imagine time flowing in a circle and your daily activities flowing right along with it, like toy boats in a whirlpool. In circular time, there is less rushing, less pressure, less anxiety. When we see time as circularly flowing, we realize that time constantly renews itself and we truly *do* have all the time in the world. Anything that doesn't happen in this moment can happen in another moment. In circular time, *time never runs out.*

The idea of circular flowing time can also be applied to the way we move through our daily activities. One popular time-saving technique is to think of your tasks as if they are on circuits and plan according to the tasks' locations — for example, tidying your house by working through adjacent rooms or running errands that are near one another on the same day. This is helpful, but in terms of establishing flow, I find that it's even more helpful to embody a circuitous approach for *internal* proximities, such as energy, creativity, intensity, or attention. To simplify this idea, let's say that there are two kinds of tasks in which you engage during the day: mindless tasks and mind-intensive tasks. If your day consists of regularly alternating between mindless tasks and highly creative tasks, you will likely lose a lot of time simply by having to change modes so many times. You'll lose time psyching yourself up for the highly creative tasks, and you'll lose time shaking off the intensity when it's time to stop being creative and move to the mindless things.

On the other hand, if you group the mindless tasks together and the mind-intensive tasks together, your brain is working much more efficiently. Even if variety is very important to you, as it is to me, by grouping tasks in logical categories, you can get much more done than you think. For example: group tasks together that require precision and accuracy; when that

Watercolor and ink on paper, 12 x 9 in.

In Time by Lucinda Pollit

group is complete, move to a group of tasks that require a lot of outgoing energy and personality (such as phone calls or correspondence). This will be much easier on your brain and imagination, and you will notice the shift very quickly, as you find yourself moving in the circular nature of flowing time. As TiCo, an ACT graduate, said, "That bridge between right and left brain can get exhausting if you do activities that make you cross it over and over and over!"

People are always looking for time-saving tips, but it's important to remember that saving time isn't like saving money. Karen Karsten, a prosperity coach and teacher, shared her thoughts on the poverty consciousness of time: "With money, you have it somewhere in a bank, in your pocket, on the dresser, and if you save it, you can see it, touch it, give it away. Not so with saved time — it just sort of disappears. I ask my clients all the time, 'How much money is enough? What would that look like?' and I think the same questions apply to time. Time is a big part of one's total prosperity."

When I'm living in the flow, I'm never trying to "save" time. Instead, I'm aiming to *conserve the energy* that can be lost rubbing against the frictional constraints of modern time while also looking to *gain energy* in time by releasing myself to more

moments of timelessness. I have a very full life, and my time is filled with many things. Yet I notice that I feel pressured and stressed only when I'm thinking about the linear clock. When I allow more flow to come into my life — not only in the freestanding, time-stopping peak experiences but also in the everyday movement of time — I feel like I am partnering with time instead of working against it, and I realize how much time there really is.

Even when we are fortunate enough to have these rich, timeless experiences of flow, we *do* have to come back into "real life." Much has been written about the importance of retreating from the modern world, but not enough has been written to instruct us on how to come back from our retreats. Whether you're returning from a meaningful vacation or from an hour of gardening or making art, I think it's helpful to recognize that coming out of flow can be a bit jarring. As with any challenge, anticipation can be a helpful tool, so plan ahead for things that might make your post-flow moments a bit easier. It is especially helpful to design ways that can help keep the experience alive. Small mementos, meaningful symbols, and talismans can serve as grounding reminders of your flow feelings and experiences, no matter where you are or what you are doing.

ARTsignment: Flow Chart

This ARTsignment helps you to pinpoint your personal flow states and create a visual motivator to engage in them more often. Here are the steps for this process:

Step 1: Answer the following journal questions to examine what "flow" means to you.

1. Describe what "losing track of time" means to you.
2. Think of a recent experience when you lost track of time. Where were you? What were you doing? Who were you with?
3. When and where are you most aware? When and where are you most awake? Most connected? Invigorated? Satisfied? Involved? What fills you with curiosity and wonder? When and where do you feel "at one" with the world?

Pick a handful of these activities, events, places, people, and things, and create a list of elements that put you in the flow state. These are the elements that you'll be using in your artwork.

Step 2: Create a piece of art, using any media or techniques, to represent the activities, events, places, people, and things that get you into the flow state. As you work on your piece, think about how you might bring more of each flow-inducing element into your life today. Look for both obvious and subtle ways to integrate these joyful states more often and more frequently.

Step 3: Place your artwork somewhere to remind you of your own personal doorway to flow, ready and waiting for you to walk through at any time!

ARTsignment Gallery: Flow Chart

Acrylic on canvas with illustrated tags, 22 x 24 in.

"I divided my canvas into eleven free-form blocks, with one flow idea per block. I doodled additional flow states in small metal-rimmed tags and then attached the tags to the back of the canvas, so that they extended down below the bottom of the canvas, like tiny pendulums of little clocks. When I first made this piece, I was living in Hawaii, and it hung in my studio, where the window was usually open. The wind streaming in from the window caused the little tags to make random clicking sounds as they hit against the wall, as if the normal tick-tock of a clock had been rearranged by improvisational jazz musicians. It was a perfect reordering of flowing time."

— MARNEY K. MAKRIDAKIS

ARTSIGNMENT GALLERY: FLOW CHART

Mixed media collage in handmade book, 6.5 x 6.5 x 1.5 in.

Front

Sample interior spread

"I made a collaged booklet from paper lunch bags. I knew I wanted to create a unique little book because it would be a portable, interactive, tangible reminder to relax. I spent a couple of weeks gathering papers, fibers, and other items around the house that represented 'flow' for me, based on my responses to the journal questions. Creating this book a little each day reminded me that I don't need lots and lots of time to forget about time. My biggest challenge is that I've always thought that the kind of peace and relaxation that comes with the disappearance of time required a lot of time to attain. In other words, I believed that the preparation of flow was too time-consuming. But this project proved to have just the opposite effect."

— L'TANYA DURANTE

ARTsignment Gallery: Flow Chart

Collage on paper, 20 x 16 in.

"I painted a background wash on watercolor paper, because I love the feel of a paintbrush in my hand. Then I collected images that represent activities (such as painting, family gatherings, sewing, meditation, and digital art projects) that put me in a 'flow' state. I even included pictures of a vacuum cleaner and a feather duster, because I love to get my space sparkly and beautiful! This process inspired me to look at ways to bring more of these flow experiences into my everyday life, to help me feel more relaxed about time. I can schedule the priorities, then incorporate some of the fun things into whatever I have to do, so all experiences are more pleasant and 'flowable.'"

— DONNA MILLS

6. CREATING TIME THROUGH GRATITUDE

Appreciating through Time

Poetic Pause

Time as winter rose
Gently folded in the snow
Supplicate in prayer

*I*n external time, objects depreciate over time. What if we could live in a way so that objects, relationships, and feelings *appreciate* over time, literally expanding their meaning through appreciation? What would it mean to measure our time by appreciation and gratitude?

In the ARTbundance training, we study nine Principles that activate self-awareness, and we call Gratitude the "core Principle," as it is the Principle on which all the others are based. Gratitude is the foundation of full, voluminous living. Gratitude is the extent to which we are fully embodying appreciation. It is also a measure of our capacity to fully embody *time*.

When I was a child, our family dinners always began with a grace that my parents created for us to all sing together. Now, as I am raising my own family, we are starting our own traditions for grace at mealtime. When Kai was not even a year old, he learned that when our little family sat down to eat and we told him it was time for grace, we all held hands. Since he got accustomed to our praising him after saying grace, he very quickly became content to keep his hands in ours for only

Grateful for Time

Answer this: in what ways are you *grateful for time*? One of the gifts of gratitude is of course the capacity to be grateful for things that challenge us. Gratitude for time allows us to move beyond the all-too-often-normal states of being indifferent to, or antagonistic toward, time, allowing new insights to come forward. ARTbundance Coach Paula Swenson expresses her gratitude for time in this way: "I am grateful that time *is*, in my experience, mutable — that it stretches and compresses and keeps everything from happening all at once. I am grateful that time is mysterious, that we don't fully understand it and therefore we must dance with it to learn more."

a few seconds and then would immediately let go, clapping his hands wildly and laughing out loud in celebration.

This adorable demonstration obviously shortened the time that we said grace, because Tony and I eventually would just start cracking up and join in Kai's celebratory antics. But this new grace, though brief in time, reminded us of what gratitude is all about. Gratitude is a time to wildly celebrate, to clap our hands and say "Yay!" for all the ordinary and extraordinary things that bless our lives. We called this quickened experience "*express* grace," a term that has become part of our family vernacular. Express grace reminds us that gratitude is qualitative, not quantitative. Grace is measured by meaning, not by minutes.

PRACTICING GRATITUDE

The word *practice* has two meanings when we think about a gratitude practice. A practice is something we do regularly, and practice also refers to the repetitive efforts made to increase proficiency and skill. A gratitude practice, then, is both a positive habit and one that, over time, makes the act of gratitude more natural, easy, joyful, and powerful.

I believe that a regular gratitude practice is one of the very best things we can do to quickly change the way we experience life. Gratitude doesn't require you to belong to any specific religion or philosophy, and it cuts across all boundaries of politics and nationality. All that is required is for you to keep your eyes, ears, and heart receptive to even the little ordinary joys around you. Feeling deep gratitude is wonderfully addictive; the more we do it, the more we *want* to do it, and so we begin looking even more deeply to reflect on things for which we're grateful.

I first learned about the amazing power of gratitude during a time when my financial situation was quite bleak, and I decided that I needed to be focusing on something else besides my empty bank account. I invented a new kind of accounting system, where I recorded all the things for which I was grateful in an old accounting ledger as a way to recognize that prosperity and abundance come in many forms. It was amazing how prosperous I felt as my daily "balance" of blessings kept getting bigger and bigger. Sure enough, before long, my outward financial picture started changing as well. I believed in this system so much that I created an

Mixed media on paper, 8.5 x 8.5 in.

Gratitude for Emergence by Peggy Lynn

online program to inspire others to try it, too, called "Accounting Your Blessings." This process made me realize that wealth is truly *perception*, and by simply analyzing prosperity through a different measurement system — through gratitude — we can make remarkable changes. We can do the same thing with time.

Here are some positive guidelines for creating a gratitude practice:

1. **Make it *consistent*.** While any kind of gratitude is good, I've noticed that the wonderful effects of gratitude *really* occur when we engage in a practice of gratitude that is regular and consistent. A specific structure that is easily replicable from day to day makes it easier to experience gratitude as a pillar in your life. For example, think about the time of day that works best, and a particular way in which you can express your gratitude easily and regularly. You might experiment and try a few different things until you find the alternative that seems the most natural.

2. **Make it *customized*.** I encourage a gratitude practice because gratitude works best when we do it rather than just think about it. A gratitude

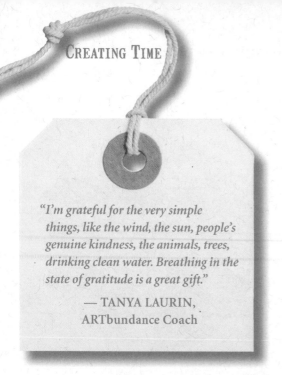

"I'm grateful for the very simple things, like the wind, the sun, people's genuine kindness, the animals, trees, drinking clean water. Breathing in the state of gratitude is a great gift."

— TANYA LAURIN,
ARTbundance Coach

practice is truly motivating when we customize it to our interests and passions. For example, creative individuals will be much more engaged when they are writing or drawing about their blessings rather than just halfheartedly thinking about them. A runner may have more success incorporating a gratitude meditation into her jogging time than she would by just entering her thoughts in a daily journal. Think of simple, doable activities that you really enjoy, and play with incorporating them into a regular gratitude practice. This is the ultimate win-win, because then you are making both gratitude *and* your favorite activities part of your daily life, blending them in a beautiful synergy.

3. **Make it *conducive*.** Your practice needs to fit in with your real life, so be realistic about what you can and cannot do, and think of ways for your practice to fit in with the nooks and crannies of what your life looks like. For example, if you don't have a lot of time to yourself because you are parenting young children, think of ways in which you might include *them* in your gratitude routine, so that you are spending high-quality time with them while also actively engaging in your gratitude practice. Or, if you have a long commute, perhaps you could use a handheld device to record a verbal list of your blessings while on the road or in the train.

4. **Make it *challenging*.** Just as a physical exercise routine needs to be changed up every now and then to challenge new muscle groups, we also need to regularly tweak our gratitude practice to keep it fresh and relevant. Your gratitude practice ought to be comfortable, easy, and doable — but not to the point that it becomes stale, mechanical, or routinized. Expressing your gratitude in new ways also opens you up to having new eyes with which you can see all kinds of new blessings that you may not have noticed before.

A gratitude practice won't work if it comes from a place of pressure, guilt, or overwhelm. The last thing a busy person needs is to think of gratitude as another "should" on her list. Rather than seeing your gratitude practice as "something else to do," I invite you to think of it as something that can *expand* your sense of time.

Gratitude bridges the entire time continuum, from the past through the present into the future. Gratitude helps us to remember what matters most, as we make the present memorable, casting a light of hopeful expectation for what is to come. In our busy day-to-day lives, we tend to focus on the big events in time rather than the quiet, moment-to-moment passages. We look toward deadlines, departures and arrivals, paydays, launch dates, and appointments, all the while forgetting that the slowly ticking clock is part of the entire time continuum. Gratitude helps us to unify the loud hourly clock chime with the soft, barely perceptible second-hand tick. It allows us to adjust our *temporal depth perception*, not only in how deeply we see time but also in how deeply it affects us. Every moment contains a gift, if we turn our attention to see it.

AN ALTERNATIVE TO MULTITASKING

What is a "moment," exactly? We all use precise definitions of seconds, minutes, and hours, but the term *moment* can describe any and all of these measurements simultaneously. I believe a moment is a snapshot that is qualitative rather than quantitative. For this reason, the moment seems to be the most apt unit of time in which to measure gratitude.

Moments allow us to extend mere minutes and expand our sense of them. When we become aware of the fullness of a given moment, we then process that moment not just mentally but also visually, aurally, tactilely, olfactorily, and intuitively. I like to think of this multilayered awareness as *multibasking*, a very appealing antidote to multitasking, which has become the default approach to time management in modern life. Multibasking is taking it all in, expanding time by expanding our appreciation of each moment.

Acrylic on canvas, 18 x 24 in.

Multibasking as Far as the I Can See
by Marney K. Makridakis

My father was ill for many years before he died, first with kidney failure and then with cancer. These diseases seemed to simultaneously harden his resolve and soften his outlook. He once shared these words with me in an email: "I am living in the indicative (When I die…) rather than the subjunctive (If I were to die…). That shift of sensibilities has added a dimension and intention to my life. As best I know my heart and mind, I am not afraid of living with illness or dying from illness. I'll take each in its own turn and on its own terms. No denials. No bargains. But a special gratitude and consolation for the living of these days, the depth of which I truly wish could be experienced by all humanity." In his last years, I watched Dad make the transition from being a multitasker to being a multibasker. He took it *all* in. He *appreciated* with time.

GRATITUDE AS A TIME MEASUREMENT

Gratitude is a lens through which we can both view and measure our life. Like time, gratitude can be measured in a variety of ways. We can comparatively measure gratitude by the "size" of the object or its source (for example, a ladybug on a leaf is small; a near-death experience is large) or by depth of feeling (a slight sense of gratitude to intense feelings of gratitude). We can even compare gratitude within the context of time (such as being grateful for a quick laugh while watching TV, as opposed to being grateful for four good years in college). No matter how we might measure gratitude, our simple awareness of it allows us to notice and reflect on the blessings in our life. In doing so, we expand our sense of time; we create more time when we focus less on how we *spend* time and focus more on what we *receive* from time.

One of the goals of this book is to help us measure time qualitatively; yet, as we've explored, this is something that we all do naturally. Nowhere is this more obvious than in our use of the terms *good time* and *bad time* to define our moments and memories. While it's completely natural to label experiences in this way, it is *gratitude* that allows us to reset these measurements at will. For example, here is one way I can describe the first few months of last year:

Those months were very difficult. The day after my husband had to leave to take care of his dying mother early in January, I broke my foot chasing after Kai. A few weeks later, I had foot

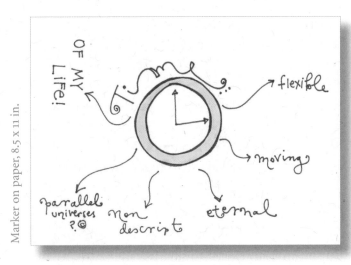

Marker on paper, 8.5 x 11 in.

Time of My Life by Leonie Dawson

surgery, and shortly after that, Kai got very sick with the flu, an ear infection, and eventually bronchitis. Then the entire city came to a virtual standstill because of severe ice storms topped off with snow, which in colder states would be laughable but which here in Dallas crippled the city and brought a slew of weather-related crises. To top it off, while still recovering from my foot surgery, I got sick, and then sicker, and I was taken to the ER after an abnormal EKG, and it turned out that I also had dehydration and pneumonia, which I ended up battling for months afterward...

That is one way I could describe the first months of last year. Here is another perfectly accurate way I could describe those same months:

- On yet another snowy day, my husband and I were staring out the sliding door thinking about the inconveniences and snow closings and such, and then little Kai, staring out the window, burst into the most joyous smile and said, "I think it's the *best* snow I ever, ever saw!" which instantly melted away our snowy worries.
- I was delighted to get to choose my own color for my foot's cast. I chose the brightest shade of orange, and it made me so happy. It might just have been the radiating neon glow, but it seemed to make everyone else lighten up a bit, too, even strangers.
- While I was having a bad coughing fit, Kai, then two years old, said to me, "Okay, take a good breath, Mommy," and his adorable compassion was as sweet as oxygen.
- My health needs prompted some major reorganization at work, which resulted in valuable, sustainable changes made for the better.
- On Valentine's Day, my sweet husband sang me a love song, and I felt the same flutter I had felt on Valentine's Day over a decade earlier.
- I made eye contact with a little bird who skipped on my windowsill, just to give me a little hop of hope.
- My friend Karen sent me a bouquet of sunflowers, "just because," without even knowing everything that had been going on with me, as I hadn't done a good job of keeping in touch.

This list could go on and on... and that is the infinity of grace. Two lists could describe the same time period. The first list, however, of "not so good things that happened," is finite, and yet my second list of little miracles feels *infinite*. Gratitude allows us to touch infinity, as we keep remembering more and more lovely moments from the past, and focusing on more surprising gifts in the present. We all get to choose what we remember about *any* swatch of time. Life certainly isn't always easy, but we can remember Kai's words to "take a good breath" and see the whole picture, the infinity of tiny ecstasies, as we live our lives, oxygenated by the little miracles everywhere around us.

ARTsignment: The GratiTimeline

This project invites you to become more aware of the role of personal gratitude in your life and to explore how gratitude influences the way you experience time.

Step 1: Schedule a day when you can commit to maintaining a conscious connection to gratitude throughout the day's waking hours. Before this day, do a little bit of preparation:

1. Prepare a pile of paper strips approximately seven inches long by one inch wide. You can cut them out of plain white paper, or colored or patterned paper. Make sure you have at least one strip for each hour that you predict you'll be awake during the day.
2. Put your strips, along with a couple of pens or markers, in a small plastic bag or other convenient receptacle.
3. Plan where you'll keep the bag so that you can access it easily throughout the day (such as in your purse or pocket).

Step 2: On your chosen day, as each waking hour passes, pick one of your slips of paper and write on it a list of all the things you're grateful for from the previous hour. You may want to set up some kind of timer to remind you when each hour has passed, or you can also just have a general awareness of the passing hours throughout the day. Either way, aim to *complete one slip per hour*, as regularly as possible, for each waking hour in the day.

Step 3: At the end of the day, gather your pile of completed strips and some tape, and spend some quiet time assembling your strips into a chain-link garland. As you string the garland together, imagine that this chain is a new kind of timekeeper: a "GratiTimeline." This timeline — both its length and the breadth of what the slips contain — is now a new way to measure your day and what you received from it.

Step 4: Answer the following journaling questions to further reflect on your experience:

1. How did you keep track of each passing hour? Did this tracking affect or change your awareness of the passage of time? (For example, did the hours seem to go more slowly or more quickly than you perceived them?)

2. In what ways did the hourly recording of gratitude affect or influence your day? What did you notice?

3. Did this concentrated gratitude exercise alter or change your experience or awareness of time in any way? If so, how?

4. Did you find that the nature of your slips changed throughout the day? For example, as the day went on, did you find that your slips contained more or fewer items? What else did you notice?

5. When you assembled the slips and reflected on your garland as a new kind of timekeeper, what thoughts and ideas came to mind? What did you notice as you viewed the GratiTimeline as a visual depiction of your day and what you received from it?

6. How might you integrate this practice into your ongoing life? For example, an hourly strip may be difficult to maintain, but could you try doing a daily strip for thirty days, to assemble a GratiTimeline for the coming month?

7. How might a regular GratiTimeline practice serve you in your life right now? How might it change the way you experience time? Imagine that you can time-travel to one year from today, and you've completed a GratiTimeline of 365 strips. How do you imagine this experience might affect you?

ARTSIGNMENT GALLERY: GRATITIMELINE

Garland of collages on paper strips, 1.5 x 36 in.

"I created my first chain-link 'journal' several years ago, as a time-saving device. When my father was ill and dying, I knew it was important to record my feelings, but I also knew I didn't have a lot of time available, so I created small collages on strips and put them together in a garland. The technique has taken many formats since then: my garlands were featured in an art magazine; I created a guided online workshop called 'The Gratitude Garland'; Artella offers a license for ARTbundance Coaches to use the Gratitude Garland in their own workshops and classes and on a personal level; and I've continued to make Gratitude Garlands — I've even made several as gifts for friends. When I was writing this book, I realized that the Gratitude Garland format was an ideal nonlinear timekeeper. With a few adjustments, the GratiTimeline was born. I love making these garlands and find that they make delightfully meaningful decorations, such as the one strewn about this little plant sitting in Artella's office window."

— MARNEY K. MAKRIDAKIS

ARTsignment Gallery: GratiTimeline

Paper strips for garland, 1 x 6 in. each

"I live in a town in the Czech Republic with a clock tower that chimes the hours, which is lovely, but also you become accustomed to it, especially if you are engrossed in something. Listening for the hourly chimes was a great exercise in mindfulness, which I try to practice but often miss. It reminded me to take breaks in a busy day and made me more productive. It reminded me of being in a monastery, with the ritual of hourly prayers. Assembling the garland was its own meditation, and I noticed that I enjoyed the rhythms of the designs and colors that reflected the changes of energy throughout the day. I think this would be a lovely daily meditation practice. I think it would be amazing to see the long lovely chain of gratitude and time stretching around the room, and I think it would be fascinating to observe the colors and designs reflecting the rhythms of my changing moods and the seasons."

— PAULA SWENSON

ARTsignment Gallery: GratiTimeline

Paper garland, 1.5 x 20 in.

"I kept track of the time by simply using an egg timer at first. After a while, however, I used my own inner clock. In the beginning of this assignment, it seemed as if the hour passed very quickly. However, as my day began to wind down, the time seemed to pass much slower. By having to stop and focus on the details of my day, I became more aware of what it was I was doing. Things that I might not have really noticed as something to be grateful for came into focus. Discovering this, I began to see how often we may say we are grateful for the bigger things in our life — family, friends, health — but I am not sure how often we stop and become grateful for the smallest things in our life: the worms that help the soil, a cool breeze on a warm day, the sound of laughter. If I did this every day, my whole house would be filled with gratitude in such a short period of time! Garlands would be hanging from ceiling to floor, and the mental picture of that makes me smile." — PATRICIA J. MOSCA

ARTSIGNMENT GALLERY: GRATITIMELINE

Paper garland, 1.5 x 49 in.

"Simply being focused on my blessings changed my whole perception of the day. Things that I normally take for granted or that frustrate me during the day took on a new meaning when I looked for the positive side of the scenario. For example, sometimes I dread mealtime with my son because it is so messy. However, on the day I created the GratiTimeline, I was appreciative of the fact that I had a refrigerator full of nutritious food for my son as well as a healthy, happy son who can feed himself (even if it includes some food throwing, too). As the day progressed, I was challenged to broaden my scope, and it opened my eyes to the big and small blessings that I take for granted every day. I want to take away from this exercise the reminder to find joy and have gratitude for all aspects of the day — including the routine, background, or supporting items that normally don't get proper attention."

— JEAN E. SIDES

7. Creating Time through Love

Traveling at the Speed of Love

Poetic Pause

Time as waltzing heart
Beats continue without thought
Drumdance of a day

One of my favorite alternative clocks is something we all have access to: the simple beating of our own heart. I find that when I'm rushing around and can feel myself in a busy fit, sometimes I just stop, put my hand on my heart, let it beat inside my chest, truly feel it, and remind myself of the ways that our hearts are connected. This quick and simple technique gets me geared back into the present, especially when I'm worried, really busy, or feeling like I'm rushing around. It immediately reminds me that *love is the ultimate keeper of time.*

I usually write Artella's biweekly e-zine right before it goes out. There was, however, one time when I wrote the e-zine a week in advance. Typically, this probably wouldn't seem so odd; for most of us, it's a pretty safe bet that anything we write right now will still be true a week from now. In our everyday life, the gap between the present and the immediate future seems small and insignificant. We're used to this fluidity from present to future; it comforts us and protects us from being too fearful of change.

However, in this instance, two-year-old Kai was to have major surgery in a few days, a total cranial reconstruction to rebuild his skull so that his brain could continue to grow properly. So, in that moment, the juxtaposition between the present and future was at once both blurry and sharply jagged, like a young child's drawing of a ferocious and absurd dinosaur. By the time my e-zine readers read the message, the surgery would be over, so writing the message felt a bit surreal, as if I were looking straight into the blinding light of the future's fragile unknown.

But was that moment really any different from any other moment? Physical science dictates that we can see everyday objects because we view the light reflected off them. If we look directly into the light source itself, our vision is distorted, and all we see are shadows and outlines. It's the same thing with *time*. Of course, we *never* know what the next moment will bring; the future can never be more than an outline. We don't know what might happen that could change everything in an instant. When we can wrap our heads around this, we slowly come to realize that for as much time as we spend worrying about it, the *future* isn't what truly matters most of all.

> "What matters most to me is the interconnectedness of all things in the infinity of time, from the smallest creature to the universe itself. The cosmic glue holding it all together is love."
>
> — SUSAN SCHIRL SMITH,
> ARTbundance Coach

While making plans for the future certainly has its place, it's no small irony that we begin to take life for granted when we start to stare *longingly* into the future's light instead of looking *lovingly* at what's right in front of us. The best way I know to avoid this and to keep focused on the beauty of what today offers is to focus on *love*.

Fast-forward through linear time, and I can now share that Kai's surgery was a total success. Those precarious days before his surgery seem so far away, and yet I can remember those tender uncertainties and swallowed tears as if they happened just this morning. Thus is the subjective nature of both time and love. In those days right before Kai's surgery, it was, of course, my love for Kai that could instantly bring me back to the sparkly, shimmering present moment. But we don't need an urgent health matter to do this all the time. We can have simple sweet love for a favorite pen, a favorite place to walk, or even the smell of the air right before and after it rains. All of these things allow us to travel at the speed of love.

Recently, after putting Kai to bed, I was reading an essay about the theory of relativity in Richard Feynman's book *Six Not-So-Easy Pieces* in which Feynman said, "The measurement of time depends on the speed at which you move." Well, as good fortune had it, I first misread it and thought it said, "The measurement of time depends on the speed at which you *love*." I laughed to myself, closed the book, and pulled Kai's baby monitor close to my ear; and I did nothing but listen to him breathe. If the measurement of time did in fact depend on the "speed" at which I was loving him just then, there's a good chance that the clocks went haywire and I'm writing this chapter to you from a point far off in the future!

But back on earth, you too can travel at the speed of love for those dearest to you and fly to the ends of the universe in your own cozy time machine. The amazing power of love has always been a much more accurate and meaningful keeper of time; our heartbeats have always chimed in tandem with the moments that define us and our deepest longings.

Mixed media clock, 12 x 12 in.

A Time for Love by Cathleen Spacil

VIEWING TIME THROUGH LOVE

When Kai had just turned two, my family was riding in the car, and as toddlers are prone to do, he sat in his car seat repeating the same made-up words over and over. In an effort to get him to move on to another "tune," Tony used the often-successful

Activating Love through Memory

In an online discussion about time and memory, one of my students, Susan McLean, wrote,

> During childhood, we enjoyed these amazing long beautiful summer days: waking to breakfast sizzling in a black iron skillet, bursting outside to swing out over Lake Erie on a tire swing hung from a weeping willow, bouncing in the waves of the lake, finding jewels of blue and green sea glass on the beach, playing cops and robbers at dusk with the fireflies lighting the night, being called in by the bell to a spaghetti dinner with corn on the cob. Then there were bonfires at night with singing and ghost stories, leading to being lulled to sleep by the sound of our giggles, the waves, and the breeze. I cherish these memories.

Remembering moments like Susan's — times when our hearts were filled with love — is a powerful way to activate love in our present. What memories come to mind for you?

tactic of distracting him with a question completely off the subject — one that Kai wouldn't know the answer to but that would quiet him for a few moments while he thought about it. Tony asked him, "Kai, what's the meaning of life?" and I barely had time to chuckle to myself before Kai left us breathless when, after only a moment's pause, he said outright, "Da meaning uv life is…I love you. Dat's da meaning uv life. Uh-huh."

Tony and I looked at each other with tears in our eyes, incredulous. From the mouths of babes, for sure! Love is the meaning of life, and *love is also the meaning of time*; love is why we are here. Living at the speed of love connects us to all three time states — past, present, and future — and helps us to see beyond the fallacy that time is only the present moment. We can extend love in *both* directions to further enhance our sense of the present moment and expand our perception of time. Consciously calling up memories of things we love helps us to bring forward more of what we love into the future. The time continuum works in our favor, as past, present, and future become one: one vibrant life measured in love.

PROBLEMS WITH PRIORITIZING

So often we feel that time is controlling us, and we forget that we *can* control time. Even if we don't always have control over the *things* we do, we have control over *how* we do them. For example, you may not have a choice right now about having to drive a long commute to work each day. However, you do have choices about how you use that time and, specifically, what you are thinking about and reflecting on during that time. It is through these choices that you can *make that time your own.*

Many time management books suggest that we get very clear about our priorities and values and then consistently make choices about our time that are in line with those priorities. This is, indeed, a great start. We start saying no to things that are not in line with our most important priorities and start saying yes to the things that are.

However, prioritizing can get us only so far. Prioritizing involves looking at "what is most important." But more often than not, the very act of evaluating "what is most important" can just lead to *more* overwhelm, as we get swallowed up in a dark, urgent, pressure-filled energy that makes us feel incapable and unconfident. This is why so many people get stuck when prioritizing, myself included.

When I am in a state of overwhelm, I finally can get things done when I focus not on "what's most important" but instead on "what is *really* most important… to me." Momentum and motivation are the two crucial keys to getting things done, and both of them are fueled solely by *what we truly love.*

EXISTING IN TWO TIMES AT ONCE

Of course, we all have things we need to do with our time, even though they aren't in line with our top priorities. Back to the commute example: A long commute may not fit in with your top priorities, but it's something you have to do. Perhaps a long-term goal might be to work toward changing jobs, but in the present moment, the commute does fill your time, even though you don't like it. When you time-travel at the speed of love, however, you learn how to *exist in two times at once.*

When you time-travel at the speed of love, your body may be in one time and place, performing the mundane task at hand, but through the focused power of love, your energy and emotions can be held elsewhere. Once again, we can look to science for several metaphorical comparisons, such as the possible existence of parallel universes, as well as theories in quantum mechanics proving that tiny atoms and molecules can effectively, albeit mind-bogglingly, be in two places at the same time. After all, it may be a while until you get to the point that your schedule is filled only with activities that are aligned with your highest priorities (and let's face it, that

Acrylic on canvas; 24 x 18 in.

Time-Traveling at the Speed of Love
by Marney K. Makridakis

may feel pretty far off from where you are now). Like the quantum molecule, however, you can exist in two places at once; even when you are doing things that aren't connected to your true loves and passions, you can still be *energetically connected* to the things that are.

This energetic connection happens when you are stuck in traffic but you are thinking warm, loving thoughts about your family. Or when you're at the doctor's office but you are reflecting on your next step in your creative dream. Or when you are washing the dishes but you are breathing deeply to fill your body with oxygen and optimum health. In other words, if you can identify your true loves and passions, not only can you make decisions about your time to reflect those priorities, but also you can make a conscious effort to *think about and reflect on those things*, no matter where you are or what you are doing, thus engaging in constant alignment with *love*...all the time!

NEW CHOICES ABOUT TIME

Once you get really clear about your true priorities, you become motivated to make new kinds of choices about how you spend your time. You start making time for what is important to you and letting go of the things that are not. Of course these changes don't happen overnight, but each time you make a choice toward something that is important to you, know that you are making excellent progress.

In chapter 3, I shared a personal memory about my dear friend Dee Dee Fields McKittrick, who received a terminal diagnosis at age twenty-five. She lived a year and a half after her diagnosis, and during that time, it was amazing to watch how she chose to use her time. Suddenly nothing else mattered but, well, the *things that mattered*! She chose her priorities and followed them: She quickly married the love of her life and decided to speak out as an advocate for AIDS awareness. She divided her time between engaging in activities she loved with people she loved and getting a lot of rest so that she could conserve her energy for the things that mattered most. The shifts she quickly made in her life continue to inspire me today and are, to me, the living proof that it is entirely possible to make dramatic shifts in the way we spend our moments, if only we'll allow ourselves to do so.

Dee Dee's story is obviously a dramatic example, but it is certainly one we can all apply to our own lives. We all have examples of times in our life when we were convinced that we didn't have time to do something, but then something happened and we were forced to make the time. For example, think of all those times when you said there was just no way you could take time off work, but then your body took over and you got sick, leaving you with no choice but to slow down and take time off. Our bodies are immensely wise this way, and they do have a way of breaking down when we don't take the time we need. The trick is to be one step ahead of our bodies, making the choice to take care of ourselves *before* we break down. The truth of the matter is that life is a "life-threatening diagnosis" for all of us. We have no way of knowing how much time we have. So we might as well realize how precious each and every moment truly is. We can create time by creating our *own* urgency to live as if every moment counts, because it does!

Two days before my father died, he made the decision to stop medical intervention. After he articulated this decision, I suddenly lost control of my emotions. I wept and wept and couldn't stop. I apologized for this, and his response was, "Please don't worry. Don't hold back. This is not the time to hold back." The truth is, in this precious life, it is *never* the time to hold back. This means we can release our full capacity to love and allow it to propel us forward. It means we can make a choice to live fully in time and through time. It means we can time-travel at the speed of love.

ARTSIGNMENT: A CHIME FOR LOVE

It makes sense that if we are going to see time in new ways, we literally need to *see* it in new ways…by creating a new, inspiring clock that aligns us with what matters most. This ARTsignment assists you in *creating time through love* by exploring the true loves of your life and designing a new time-measuring tool to measure them.

Step 1: Answer these journal questions to explore your true loves and passions:

1. Following is a list of common core values or life experiences. Without thinking about it too much, give each item a number rating between 1 and 10, based on how *alive* and *full of love* you feel when you read it, with 10 indicating great feelings of love and aliveness:

Self-expression	Simplicity
Family	Service to society
Well-being	Freedom
Environment	Exploration
Insight	Security
Connection	Influence
Spirituality	Recognition
Achievement	Fairness
Community	Tradition
Integrity	Fun
Independence	Other: _____
Creativity	

2. Which three items have the highest numbers? (If more than three are tied, select your top three.) Does your answer surprise you? Why or why not?

3. What makes you happiest in life? What truly brings you joy?

4. What qualities do you admire most in other people?

5. What do you admire most in yourself?

6. What fills your heart with love?

7. When do you feel connected to your true passions?

8. When you are doing something you don't like doing, where do you generally *wish* you were, instead?

9. After answering these questions, review your "top three" from number two, and if necessary, revise your original response to create a new list of your top one to three love sources…the "loves of your life" that serve as your truest motivators.

Step 2: Design your own Chime for Love: a new time-telling device that celebrates the things that are most important to you. For example, I made a clock with ruby slippers (paying homage to "There's no place like home" from *The Wizard of Oz*) to celebrate *home* and *family*, which I determined as my top love sources.

Mixed media assemblage, 6 x 6 x 1.5 in.

There's No Place and Time Like Home
by Marney K. Makridakis

Step 3: Keep your Chime for Love clock someplace where it will remind you of your wonderful ability to exist in two times at once. The clock on the wall may indicate that you're in your cubicle at work, but A Chime for Love indicates that your *energy* is with your true loves and passions, right where it should be!

121

ARTsignment Gallery: A Chime for Love

Mixed media journal page, 7 x 7 in.

"My clock is measured in thirteen hours in a day, the extra hour representing gratitude. It reminds me that my true passion is in expressing myself as an artist. I have selected various states of being to remind myself that there is always time for the most important issues and values in my life. Each hour I remind myself to take time to cherish moments, and consequently I actively show up and participate in my life."

— MARILYN HARRIS MILLS

ARTsignment Gallery: A Chime for Love

Digital collage

"I love the idea of measuring time by how much joy I feel, and I loved creating a clock to do so! The clock depicts the things most important to me. These are my family, the process of self-expression, and connection. The writing prompts helped me whittle away all the extraneous excuses that prevented me from being proactive and positive in terms of how I think about and use time." — SHARON B. GORBERG

ARTsignment Gallery: A Chime for Love

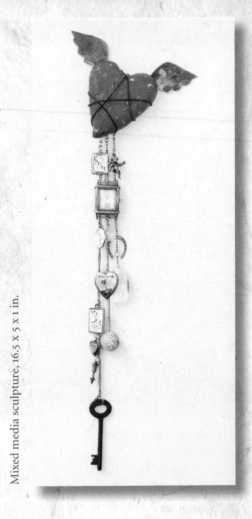

Mixed media sculpture, 16.5 x 5 x 1 in.

"My piece is titled *Time Flies*. I created it as a simple daily reminder of the little things. Every day I will wind the watch that my husband gave me twenty-three years ago. I will take this time to pause and look at all of the tiny trinkets that are so precious to me, each reminding me of special times. This will become my daily ritual of savoring time, my family, and the simple things, a daily acknowledgment of how quickly time flies!"

— MICHELLE BERLIN

8. CREATING TIME THROUGH RITUAL

Punctuating a Day

Poetic Pause

Time as crisp creases
Ancient origami dreams
Commit to each fold

W e can observe countless examples of rich traditions throughout time in which the passage of time is noted, honored, and celebrated through the practice of *ritual*. In our own communities, we all celebrate rituals that pay homage to the passage of time, even though we may not think of them as such: parades for Little League baseball, the annual arrival of a favorite seasonal vegetable at the market, Independence Day fireworks, prom nights, harvest festivals, neighborhood block parties, grand opening events, and anniversaries of every shape and form. On the personal level, ritual punctuates meaning in our daily life through celebrations of birthdays, anniversaries, holidays, and religious and secular occasions.

Ritual traditions run deep in other cultures. In the Iroquois tradition, the "good morning

> *"Does it ever really matter that I am 'late' and 'behind'? No, what matters is that I do my best and, with good grace and presence, be where I am right now. Ritual lets me pay more attention to this state of being; I'm paying attention to what I'm paying attention to."*
>
> — SIAN POPE, ARTbundance Coach

Watercolor and gold leaf cn paper, 13 x 18 in.

Harvest Moon by Paula Swenson

message" is a daily thanksgiving ritual, delivering a salute to Mother Earth and all her beauty. The Balinese have about a dozen life cycle rites that are performed throughout a child's early life at certain designated time intervals (such as the seventh, twelfth, thirty-fifth, and forty-seventh days of a child's life), and they celebrate many other special rituals, such as the Mesangih teeth-filing rite for welcoming adulthood. African societies celebrate significant points of the life cycle by offering gifts to ancestral spirits; people often leave baskets of food on the ancestral burial ground. During the three years I lived in Hawaii, I was incredibly moved by the many rituals that have been passed down through centuries from early Polynesian culture, marking the seasons and other important events in time. These are just a few examples of the strong presence of ritual that exists across cultures, across time.

RITUAL AND TIME

Rituals allow opportunities for attention, recognition, and celebration; they also provide opportunities for us to personalize and control our experience of creating time. Ritual helps us to frame time, as a photograph or painting that is framed visually "pops" and is given its proper due. In the same way, rituals allow us to *frame* time so that our experience bursts through the linear aspects of our days and creates a fourth dimension for time, the axis for which is, simply, meaning.

The world is full of time-honored rituals; we can also *create rituals that honor time.* If we are feeling lost and disjointed in life, regularly engaging in rituals anchors us back in the *now.* We can even create in-the-moment rituals whenever we are having a "bad time" — that is, when we are doing something that we are not necessarily enjoying. Even something as mundane as housekeeping can be elevated to another experience, as one of my students, Bheki Naylor, discovered. She shares,

I was exhausted, bored, and I ached for something magical. I was aiming to create a new work area for my art, and it felt heavy and like work instead of fun. Then I realized I was calling it a "work space"; no wonder I felt like all I ever did was work — I made everything out to be work! So I designed a new ritual of creating a sparkly, magic-filled space: instead of "cleaning," I'm "sparkle-crafting." In engaging in my new ritual, I've realized how time and space are so closely related. If I can create a sparkly, magic-filled space, then I can also manipulate time to be sparkly and magic filled.

Paula's Story: Time and the Sema Ritual

"My experience with formal rituals is best illustrated by the *sema,* the circular dance-prayer of the Sufi dervishes. It is an amazing and beautiful ritual that includes drums, flutes, vocalization, and of course the 'whirling' of the dervishes. The musicians enter first, into a gallery to the side; the drums begin; then the hypnotic breathy vocalizations, followed by the haunting flute sounds of the ney. The dervishes enter the sacred space in their tall hats and dark robes; one by one they shed their dark outer garments to reveal the white robes of purity. Each movement is part of the ritual; each has meaning. As an observer, you might not understand the specific meaning, but you are aware of a very focused sense of purpose: the placing of the hand on the heart, the tilt of the head, the totality of the focus of the dervishes. I've been fortunate enough to watch this haunting ritual more than half a dozen times, and each time I am transfixed by the sense of total immersion in the moment, the sense of there being only *now.* The sema lasts as long as it takes. It has no prescribed length. When it is complete, I have no sense at all of how much time has passed because I have been fully engaged in the present." — Paula Swenson

Rae's Story: Time and the Holy Sabbath Ritual

Watercolor and ink on paper, 14 x 11 in.

Shabbos is the Soul of the world. Shabbos gives us the power to elevate Time to Holiness. Six days of the week we work to separate the Holiness out of the weekdays, by doing good, staying away from evil, sifting the Holy Sparks that were hidden in the week. Then everything is elevated on SHABBOS.

Shabbos is unchanging, eternal. The weekdays are constantly changing, up and down, up and down. But on Shabbos, everything is complete.

Shabbos Soul by Rae Shagalov

"From sundown Friday to an hour after sundown on Saturday, I, along with all other Orthodox Jews, observe Shabbos Kodesh, or Holy Sabbath, a ritual that elevates the mundane work of the whole week into holiness. This is a very holy day, and the quality of the day feels completely different from that of the rest of the week. When people who do not observe the Sabbath come to my house on the Sabbath, they tell me that they feel like they are entering and leaving a different time — and they are right! The Sabbath is expressly set aside to be a full day of being in the world versus *acting* on the world. It is a day for appreciating creation rather than being creative.

"It begins when Jewish women all over

continued on next page

As Bheki's story demonstrates, we can use ritual to find the magic in anything, in any time. Rituals *create time* much the way that snowflakes are created in one of the most breathtaking demonstrations of nature. Paul Douglas wrote in his book *Restless Skies*, "Snow crystals are really soil particles that have been dressed up in an icy cloak." Science shows that snowflakes are actually made from many separate snow crystals, all of which have formed around small bits of dirt. Through this awe-inspiring transformation, dirt becomes a gorgeous quilt of nature's lace, decorating the trees, giving birth to joy-filled snow angels and sleigh rides, and finally kissing us on the nose, greeting us in innocence and delight. Similarly, rituals can wrap themselves around the otherwise mundane, earthy, dusty, granular moments of our lives and make them sparkle, lifting them up into the heavens before they dance right into our laps, reminding us how grateful we are to be alive.

CREATIVE BIRTH DAYS

In my work with creative people, I often suggest initiating rituals to honor *all* the births in our life, including the birth of a new creative project. Commemorating the "birthday" of a new project sends a message — to our subconscious mind, to our friends, to our inner critics — that says, "This is important to me and my time." By engaging ritual, we invite spirit and practicality into a timeless sisterhood to support optimal creative success. A birthday ritual recognizes the bittersweetness of labor and delivery, and it provides a natural timeline for tracking progress. It also can reduce overwhelm, making the beginning of a project feel joyful and fun instead of draining and difficult. By honoring a new project with a special ritual, we give the project the gift of our time and attention, setting the stage for continuing commitment to create the time for this project as it evolves.

Here are a few suggestions of ways in which you might honor the birth of a new creative project:

continued from previous page

the world light Shabbos candles eighteen minutes before sundown on Friday to usher in the Divine light and peace of the Sabbath. The Jewish people honor and delight in the holy day through ritual such as prayer, learning Torah, feasting with family and friends, and refraining from everyday work. When three stars appear in the night sky on Saturday, we then separate from the Sabbath and bring this new level of holiness into the work week ahead. The Sabbath ritual supports Jewish time as more than just a linear flow of minutes; it is a spiral of time, ever ascending in holiness."
— Rae Shagalov

- Buy a beautiful candle to keep in your creative space as your "birthday candle." Light it each time you begin a work session on your project.
- Send a "birth announcement" to your friends, announcing your new project.
- Take yourself on a birthday adventure outdoors. Pick up items that catch your eye — a leaf, a shell, a lucky penny. Put them in a special place where you will be able to cherish them as special birthday gifts for your project.
- Continue to celebrate subsequent anniversaries as a way to enliven the sense of magic, mystery, and expansiveness of what you have birthed into being.

The same suggestions given here can be applied to *any* literal or figurative life passage, such as the beginning or ending of a relationship, moving into or out of a home, or the oft-neglected middle stage of any project or endeavor. Rituals truly enrich us, as we realize that each day is not just time to be passed but a gift of time to be *sacredly received*.

PUNCTUATING THE DAY WITH RITUAL

Being stressed or anxious about time tends to especially affect us at the beginning and the end of the day. In the morning, our numb bodies move through the early-day brain fuzz, and we think, "Oh gosh, how am I going to get through this day?" At night, we feel panicked and stressed, reviewing all the things that didn't get done, and our minds race through mental lists filled with self-judgment. Is this any way to live? I can't think of a bigger waste of time than allowing our precious gift of life to be diminished into a long string of stressed-out mornings and anxious evenings. And yet it's a pattern that becomes all too easy to fall into.

Mixed media on wood panel, 12 x 12 x 1 in.

Breathing Ritual by Cheryl Ball

As always, the first step to making a change is awareness about what is and is not working. After she completed the ARTsignment in this chapter, K. Lee Mock commented, "I usually begin my mornings well, so I wondered why I had been choosing to end my nights so poorly: whiny, on the couch, exhausted. This question made me face myself and this choice." To change our patterns, we must take action, and it all begins with a simple choice to do so. Taking back control of the beginning and ending of your days is one of the most powerful things you can do to reshape your relationship with time and see your days as more than just time passing. Engaging in self-designed rituals is an effective, inspiring way to connect and commune with a larger, enlightening perspective of time.

The ARTsignment in this chapter invites you to create new rituals to punctuate your days. Ideally, a ritual is simple, fun, motivating, easily replicable, and flexible. Here are a few helpful guidelines to keep in mind as you create your rituals:

- **Build the ritual from what you need.** Rather than creating a ritual for ritual's sake, design a process that directly addresses your personal needs. Start by identifying the challenges that you experience with time,

Ink on paper, 11 x 8.5 in.

Sketch from an Evening Art Walk by K. Lee Mock

and explore how ritual might help you *create time* to better serve you. When K. Lee Mock identified her biggest challenge as exhaustion at the end of the day, she designed a ritual to address it directly: "I created a ritual to walk through my neighborhood at night to release stress and inhale rejuvenation and inspiration. I carry a tiny notebook with me, just in case I want to jot down a description or draw a sketch. This ritual helps me view time as a guiding and supportive friend rather than a harsh enemy that denies me love, energy, and affection."

- **Keep it simple.** Rituals don't need to be elaborate. They certainly can be, but simple rituals are generally easier to continue and sustain. You may find that at times you respond better to more elaborate, extensive rituals, and at other times, a briefer interlude does the trick. Angela George shared her creative, yet simple, solution to the challenge of keeping up with an elaborate practice:

For years, I was quite disciplined and practiced my spiritual practice — called *sadhana* — every morning for at least thirty minutes, but these days, my morning *sadhana* is usually only practiced a few times a week. If I go more than a couple of days without *sadhana* time, I find myself stressed, tired, and irritable. So I created a piece of artwork that would anchor my yoga experiences, and my new ritual is to briefly connect with the artwork on days when I can't do my full yoga practice. When I see the artwork, I am able to go back into that relaxed state of being fairly quickly.

- **Rituals do not need to be serious to be sacred.** Have fun and allow yourself to try things that are unconventional, and even a bit silly. One of my students, Allegra Harrington, has a daily ritual in which she connects with "organizational fairies" during her lunch hour. This simple ritual allows her to step away from the office and organize her daily priorities in a fun way that always puts a smile on her face. She says, "I go to my car during lunch hour, play dreamy music, decorate the car with a little sparkle on the dashboard, and close my eyes to relax, inviting the organizational fairies to join me as we attend to my priorities. This helps me to see things more clearly, and also not take myself so seriously."

- **Build in flexibility.** Rituals work best when they are flexible opportunities rather than rigid requirements. When Cheryl Ball did the ARTsignment in this chapter, she discovered the importance of flexibility:

> I had a picture in my mind that I could sit quietly in a comfy chair or on the sofa, and just close my eyes and breathe while giving thanks. In my vision nobody was around, and I had solitude; but that's not usually true in real life. I had to let go of what I thought my ritual *should* look like and not get agitated when it wouldn't happen that way. I became more flexible and just took the opportunities when they presented themselves. Sometimes it only happened in the bathroom as I was getting ready for the day, but I would take the time to make it happen: just close my eyes, breathe, and empty my mind.

ARTSIGNMENT: A NEW RITUALITY

In this ARTsignment, you will be guided to create a new ritual to punctuate your days, and to create a piece of artwork to illustrate your New Rituality for yourself.

Step 1: Answer the journal questions below to explore how you might use ritual to punctuate your days, honor time, and commune with and from your soul.

1. What is your typical morning routine, right now? Where did this routine come from? What patterns, ideas, beliefs, and habits is it based on?
2. How would you *most like to feel* in the morning?
3. What kind of ritual could you create to help you feel this way each morning? Brainstorm a list of your ideas, welcoming whatever thoughts and ideas come to mind.
4. Select the ritual you'd like to try first. Why does it in particular seem to call to you?
5. Can you picture yourself doing this ritual each morning? Do you need to simplify it to make it easier? Do you need to make it more fun or inspiring, so that you're more motivated to do it?
6. What is your typical evening routine, right now? Where did this routine come from? What patterns, ideas, beliefs, and habits is it based on?
7. How would you *most like to feel* in the evening?
8. What kind of ritual could you create to help you feel this way each evening? Once again, brainstorm a list of raw, uncensored ideas.
9. Select the evening ritual you'd like to try first. Which one did you choose? Why does it in particular seem to call to you? Can you picture yourself doing this ritual each evening? Do you need to simplify it to make it easier? Do you need to make it more fun or inspiring, so that you're more motivated to do it?
10. How do you feel about the prospect of adding these rituals to your life? Excited? Nervous? Skeptical? Overwhelmed? Make note of how you are feeling now.

Step 2: Once you have determined the new rituals that you would like to engage in, create a piece of artwork to illustrate at least one of the rituals.

Step 3: Place the artwork in a prominent location to inspire you to engage in your New Rituality. You may even want to incorporate the piece of art into your ritual somehow. For example, each evening you might connect with your New Rituality artwork as a way to ground you to the present moment and connect you with your divine creativity.

Step 4: After giving these rituals a try for a few days, go back and adjust as necessary to make the rituals more helpful, fun, doable, practical, and inspiring.

ARTsignment Gallery: A New Rituality

Mixed media on canvases, 4 x 4 x 1.5 in. each

"I must say this exercise has made me rethink my perception of time. I made a gratitude shrine with two canvases hinged together: one with a collage and one with a small gift, reminding me to be thankful for the gift of time. It stands on my bedside cabinet where I can see it both on waking and retiring to bed, as a reminder to say a little prayer. This ARTsignment guided me to take the time to contemplate what makes prayer and gratitude meaningful to me, and now I know I will be motivated to keep on doing it! The new way to see time is very empowering, and has dissolved much fear and panic."
— LARA GEACH

ARTsignment Gallery: A New Rituality

Acrylic on canvas, 18 x 24 in.

"Several years ago, I made a new intention to start my day earlier, with some quiet time just for me before anyone else woke up. I love sunrises, and so I created a ritual to connect and commune with the rising sun. This was far more motivating to me than simply waking up early according to a number on the clock. Awakening became all about having a play date with the sun! I created this painting, which says "Watching the *fun* rise," as a reminder of my choice to connect to the *joy* in the coming day. Even if I don't always wake up early enough to see the sunrise, I can still connect to the joyful, playful energy of the new day, and the painting reminds me to do this."

— MARNEY K. MAKRIDAKIS

ARTsignment Gallery: A New Rituality

Mixed media on fabric, 16 x 12 in.

"My artwork represents my simple ritual of connecting to breath and gratitude for a few minutes every day. It is a portrait of energy and power manifesting from the universe. This ritual has gone from an "inside" meditation to an outside/inside sensory experience of appreciation and thrill and tears. It's changed my attention to my body and breathing. It has helped me expand my understanding and experience of time and energy so that I may be more present with love, positivity, and pleasure."

— SIAN POPE

9. CREATING TIME THROUGH STILLNESS

Taking a Time Out

Poetic Pause

Time as just nothing
A white in absence of hue
Still antithesis

We tend to associate time with motion, yet time can also be connected to *stillness*. Think of expressions like *quiet time*, *downtime*, *time out*, and the like. We may not be able to stop time, but we often forget that we can, however, *stop*.

Do you ever eat when you are not really hungry? I know that sometimes I have a tendency to eat just because the food is there. I think we often schedule our time in the same way. We fill hours because they are there, not paying attention to what we're filling them with. We are so used to this habit that we forget what *really* nourishes us. To get back in touch with ourselves and what nourishes us, we have to first actually *stop*. We must have some amount of open, free time each day when we are simply able to connect to ourselves. It could be as little as five or ten minutes to simply do nothing, except give our souls some empty time to just *be*.

It has been said that music happens in the silences between the notes. I'm not a chess player, but I've heard that the game of chess truly occurs *between* the moves. When I train ARTbundance Coaches, we talk about how the real coaching happens in the silences, in the pauses when the client makes her own discoveries. In all three cases, the act of pausing *allows* for necessary processing. The mere act of *stopping* changes time itself, prompting a sensation of a suspension of time that allows all other moments to become even more meaningful.

While we may not be able to stop time, we can stop *within* time. For example, if you simply took some time to stop and do nothing, you might:

- Look around you and inside you
- Listen within you and outside of you
- Allow your mind to wander and see where it goes
- Befriend your intuition
- Meditate and clear your mind of all thoughts
- Focus on one word that has meaning for you (for example, simply close your eyes and think about breathing "joy" in and out)
- Make new connections between things and ideas
- Breathe deeply; focus on your breath and nothing else
- Notice ordinary and extraordinary details around you
- Recall a meaningful memory and let it live again through you
- Really do nothing at all

Stillness is the ultimate energy generator. The personal recalibration that occurs during stillness creates more time and energy for what matters most to us.

INSPIRATION OVERLOAD

"Being still is a rejuvenating experience. We can't possibly be at our highest level of productivity unless we first connect with our source of power: the source that sustains our passion and drive to take inspired action daily. Consistent practice that nurtures connection in this way is of vital importance."

— JOZETTE RODRIGUEZ,
ARTbundance Coach

Taking time to *stop* in small ways each day opens a window for space and time to flow. Furthermore, the simple gesture of stopping all activity for five to ten minutes each day makes it easier to take those bigger leaps to stop other activities that do not serve us.

Like driving a car, living a full life of meaning consists of a combination of both accelerating and braking. Yet the latter is often neglected. We tend to think that if we add more and more inspiring and enjoyable things to our life, then our life will get more inspiring and enjoyable. Yet often that is not the case, as adding more inspiration, spirituality, and creativity can some-

times result in inspiration overload. We look around at all our inspiring books, CDs, retreats, and seminars, and at our journals filled with our dreams…and we wonder why we're still discontented. With all this evidence around us of what is possible, why does it feel so *impossible*?

As well as adding *more* inspiration to our life, we also must simultaneously put the brakes on things that do not truly serve us. This includes tasks, commitments, and relationships that drain our energy, and it also often includes elements that may be helpful and inspiring in general but don't necessarily serve us in this moment. Releasing energy drains and extraneous inspirations allows space for new inspiration. The interior space that comes with releasing extraneous elements is the most fruitful creative gift we can give ourselves.

A Lesson from Kai: Roll Down the Window

On an evening last summer, Kai, Tony, and I were driving home from dinner, and Kai asked from his car seat, "Can you roll down the window? I want to see something." Since it was unbearably hot in the midst of a Texas heat wave, we explained that the air conditioner was on and asked him what he needed to see. Kai answered, "To see how wonderful the world is." Of course, we had no choice but to roll down the window, realizing that some things are more important than air conditioning, even on a hot day.

We create wonder whenever we create the time to stop and watch the world. Wherever we are, we all can benefit from purposefully rolling down the window, even in life's blazing heat, to get glimpses of how wonderful the world can be and how we can live most fully within it.

RESISTANCE AND AWARENESS

For some people, the idea of a daily practice of stopping for stillness is unthinkable; they can always find something more important to do than "doing nothing." In truth, though, there is nothing more important than nourishing ourselves. ARTbundance Coach Athena George explained how her ideas about doing nothing have changed since having cancer: "Prior to having cancer, I thought there was no time for stopping and doing nothing. I believed that only weak, unproductive people stop. Now I know this is not the case. I love the idea of creating a practice of daily open time when I will just doodle, or close my eyes and allow my biggest wishes and dreams to unfold. It will add consistency and regularity to my schedule, with something I'm looking forward to."

Similarly, artist Patricia J. Mosca shared these words:

When I think about stopping and doing nothing, the first thing that comes to mind is the word *lazy*! I suppose that would have come from a belief I have held on to since childhood. It is easy and natural for me to be busy, to live my life in the "a busy worker is a happy worker" theme. But if I could develop a consistent and regular practice of "doing nothing" each day, I believe it might center me more. I can imagine that my life might actually run smoother if I could stop a couple times a day and just connect with my spirit to find contentment: meditate in the morning before coffee, stop in the middle of the day and take a walk in nature, or simply sit outside and listen to the sweet songs of the birds or smell the scent of freshly mowed grass, breathing it all in.

Patricia's words hint at the fact that we all need empty time to figure out *who we are and what we are meant to do*. How can we know how to best spend our time if we don't even know ourselves? How can our intuition help us when we need to make important decisions if we're not used to paying attention to it on a daily basis?

Not too long ago, I was a typical small-business owner who worked full, long days, seven days a week. It was work that I truly enjoyed, so I assumed this was acceptable, and I thought myself very fortunate. After all, it wasn't like I was slaving away in a job with no meaning or passion. This business meant the world to me — it was my baby! Well, then I *did* have a baby, and there I was, with two children: my new infant son and my feisty growing business.

Mixed media art journal page, 7 x 7 in.

Stop and Watch by Marilyn Harris Mills

Eventually, after fragmenting my time and attention, I realized that I needed to take weekends off from work to focus on my family. This greatly expanded my presence in the moment, it increased my overall productivity during the workweek, and my entire family thrived when I "put us in the bubble." I no longer felt pulled in two directions, as I did when I was trying to do it all, all the time.

Pen and ink on paper, 8.5 x 11 in.

When Time Doesn't Fly by Lanette Breedt

Once my family and I adjusted, I realized that it was not enough. I was so focused on my family all weekend that there was still no time that was just for me. I made what felt like an extreme decision: to take Fridays off from work while my son was in nursery school and make Fridays just for me. In this way, I now also put *myself* in the bubble, with a full day to attend to my own needs, including several hours of open, unplanned time.

Within the first few weeks of this significant change, all kinds of new, out-of-nowhere opportunities came my way: unexpected clients, contact from friends I hadn't heard from in ages, and even the initiation of the publishing contract for this very book you're reading. Delighted by the influx of new opportunities, I realized that, in essence, life was waiting until I had time and space for these new opportunities. After all, I didn't have time to write a book, so why would the universe send me a publishing opportunity? When I gave myself permission to have open and unplanned time, a little window reflected that opening and allowed new gifts to come forward.

I initially had deep resistance to the idea of a four-day workweek. I worried about my productivity: how could I get all my work done? I worried about my parenting: was it acceptable for my son to be in school if I wasn't working? I confess that I also worried about what other people would think. My long-standing association with the ideals of working hard reared its persistent head. I was afraid that people would think I was lazy or, worse, entitled. I was delighted to find that, instead, I inspired others to create new time and space for themselves as well.

Acrylic on canvas, 10 x 10 in.

Time Out by Marney K. Makridakis

THE ART OF UNPLANNING

Creating time when we are not worried about time is as essential as breathing. The word *inspire* means "to breathe in." How can we be inspired when we have no time to slowly breathe in? As when people on diets retrain their awareness to learn when they are truly hungry, open spaces of time allow us to learn who we really are and what we really want to do. To facilitate this, we need more than just downtime. We need time that is completely free, not only from activity but also from our own expectations.

To practice this, I invite you to engage in the art of *unplanning*: purposefully unplanning parts of your days so that absolutely nothing is scheduled, anticipated, or even *envisioned*. Whether you unplan a chunk of ten minutes in your afternoon or unplan an entire day, the cornerstone of your unplanned time is that it is just that: *unplanned*. Resist the temptation to come to your unplanned times with a mental to-do list (for example, "I have thirty minutes, so I'll meditate for ten minutes, then draw for ten minutes, and then take a ten-minute walk). Even if the things on your list are enjoyable and relaxing, the very fact that you are holding on to an agenda overrides the rich opportunity for your intuition to speak to you in the moment, guiding you in natural rhythm.

Instead, come to your unplanned times without any expectations or anticipations. Simply *show up to the moment*; close your eyes, breathe, and follow your

Unplanning and Peripato

My husband's ancestors are from the island of Crete in Greece. There, a cornerstone of daily life is *peripato*, which means "walking around." Most often, peripato happens after a meal and involves strolling without any intention or purpose; it is a simple time for thinking, dreaming, and philosophizing, perhaps in subtle connection to the age-old philosophical underpinnings of the country itself.

Like peripato, unplanning promotes *receptive* time rather than active time. In unplanning, you withdraw your will and your preconceived vision. You allow your mind to take a stroll without having any intention or purpose. In doing so, you give voice to your intuition and the timeless whispers of your heart.

heart's desire. You may end up "doing something" in your moment of doing nothing. For example, your quiet time may lead you to take a walk to the park, doodle with crayons, or stretch and breathe into your body. These inclinations are to be welcomed and embraced, provided that they come from the inspiration in the moment rather than your preconceived ideas about what your unplanned chunk of time will look like. It is a subtle distinction but an important one.

ARTsignment: Stop. Watch.

Even if you agree that unplanning and taking time each day for stillness is important, it's often challenging to follow up by acting on the concept, especially when the pace of real life wants to intercede. This ARTsignment invites you to create a new timepiece to serve as a reminder: it's called a Stop. Watch.

Step 1: Answer the following journal questions:

1. When you think about stopping and doing nothing, what comes to mind?
2. Where might these thoughts, beliefs, ideas, or associations come from?
3. What excites you about developing a consistent, regular practice of doing nothing for some time each day?
4. What resistances do you have about developing a consistent, regular practice of doing nothing for some time each day?
5. Is it easier for you to be still or busy? Why?
6. If you were to stop right now and do nothing, what might that look like?
7. If you integrated unplanned time into every day, what changes might you see in your life?

Step 2: Incorporate ideas and concepts from your answers into your creation of a Stop. Watch., a new timepiece created with any media and supplies you like, which serves as a physical reminder to *stop* your activities and *watch* the guidance from your intuition. As you work to create it, imagine how your life might change if you were to adopt this daily practice.

Step 3: Put your new creation in a place where you will see it at least once a day. When you see it, *take your time* to *Stop*. And *Watch*. Now is the time to reacquaint your soul with stillness. It's amazing how productive doing nothing can be.

ARTsignment Gallery: Stop. Watch.

Acrylic on vintage map and canvas, 18 x 24 in.

My Stop. Watch. is a reminder of how far I can travel when I just stay still. I painted directly on the surface of an old map, symbolizing the vast journeys of imagination that occur when I allow myself to do nothing but dream. Floating within the map is my very favorite place to be still: a comfy, oversized chair. I initially contemplated decorating the border with little free-form clocks, but realized that swirls more aptly illustrate the role of timekeeping during true stillness.

— MARNEY K. MAKRIDAKIS

ARTsignment Gallery: Stop. Watch.

Watercolor and ink on paper, 12 x 9 in.

"Time disappeared while I was working on this project, and I was reminded to incorporate more *enjoyment* into the things that I do. Even the mundane things like laundry and grocery shopping could go by easier by incorporating enjoyment into them. Time is a perception versus an actual thing, and by incorporating pleasure into it, my perception of it will change and improve." — DAVID WAGENFELD

ARTsignment Gallery: Stop. Watch.

Colored pencil and marker on paper, 15 x 11 in.

"I am most definitely changed by this experience. Time no longer owns me. I became aware of every moment and realized that the stillness in between the ticks and tocks matters, so we must breathe it in and revel in it. My timepiece for this project focuses on living life in the stillness between the ticks of the clock. It's time to wake up to the gentle tinkling sound of grace pouring over us. There are no hands on this clock, as soul matters in the time between the clicks. Instead of numbers, time encompasses blissful states of being."

— CHELLE SAMANIEGO

ARTSIGNMENT GALLERY: STOP. WATCH.

Watercolor and ink on paper, 9 x 9 in.

"I first started to create a clock with various things I might meditate upon, but then it got so cluttered with words that it felt way too busy — just the opposite of creating a spacious moment that was not filled with busyness. So, instead, I created a clock that was empty inside, spacious and pregnant with possibility: a vast moment, a delicious emptiness, waiting to be entered and experienced. It will be helpful to use this Stop. Watch. to remember to tune in to the infinite moment any time I am feeling stressed, busy, or pressured."

— RAE SHAGALOV

10. CREATING TIME THROUGH METAPHOR

What Color Is Your Time?

Poetic Pause

Time as time alone
Oblivious to compare
Laughing at contrast

Not long ago, I was reading a pop-up book to Kai, and it suddenly became very clear that while there are many quotes and platitudes about life being like a book, what we really need is for life to be like a pop-up book. When you're looking at a pop-up book, each page is a sensation to experience. You don't worry about how many pages are left or think about what's to come. You stop to take it all in, inserting yourself into the picture, finding treasures in all the three-dimensional nooks and crannies. "Yes…*that* is what life should be," I realized, as I snuggled closer to my sweet-smelling boy, who thankfully has not yet learned to view time as something we are supposed to worry about.

Seeing time in a new way means we can fully insert ourselves into the most beautiful pop-up page of wonder and possibility that the day can offer. When we open ourselves to this awareness, the day and all its precious pages will come to life, just as we, in turn, become fully alive in the pages ourselves. The idea of life as a pop-up book is a metaphor that helps me to design my days, and design my *time*, in a full, three-dimensional way, in which I'm living fully instead of flatly. The metaphor of the pop-up book helps me to change the way I see and experience time.

Our lives are poetic novels, filled with the metaphors we choose day by day, moment by moment. The more we understand about life, the less there is to say, as communication itself wanes in importance next to the quiet apprehension of truth. When an experience is profound, words often feel so inadequate; thankfully we have metaphors to extend the reach of meaning.

Julie's Story: Life as Swimming

Mixed media on paper, 11 x 8.5 in.

Flowing through Life
by Julie Proctor

"My metaphor for life is swimming: I flow through life with buoyancy reaching my full potential; my reach propels me forward in the water and my breath creates buoyancy, lifting me in the water. When I apply this metaphor to time, I can envision time flowing all around me. When I am overwhelmed from the pressures of time, I breathe and reach for the next stroke. I am lifted up and buoyed, mindful of the present, relaxing into the future."   — Julie Proctor

BUILDING YOUR METAPHOR MUSCLES

Thinking metaphorically becomes more natural and automatic the more you do it. One way to build your metaphor muscles is to reflect on the poetic pause at the beginning of each chapter in this book. As recommended in the book's introduction, I invite you to extend the moment even further and reflect on its meaning, not only in this moment but through time. For example:

- What does the poem make you remember? (past)
- How does the poem make you feel right now? (present)
- What wishes or dreams come to mind? (future)

I also encourage you to compose your own poetic pauses. This is a great way to try on different metaphors as you pause and absorb what you are reading.

For further experimentation with metaphors, I invite you to try the Metaphor Machine, a fun tool I invented for creative writers. It's a whimsical progression of exercises where you begin with any word, and once you run it through the graphical map of the Metaphor Machine, you end up with twenty-four new words, phrases, and images to work with. Here is an example, using the word *white*:

> *"Time is like a lava lamp, organic and yet electric, somewhat predictable yet ever changing, always peaceful and still intriguing."*
>
> — DANA SEBASTIAN-DUNCAN,
> ARTbundance Coach

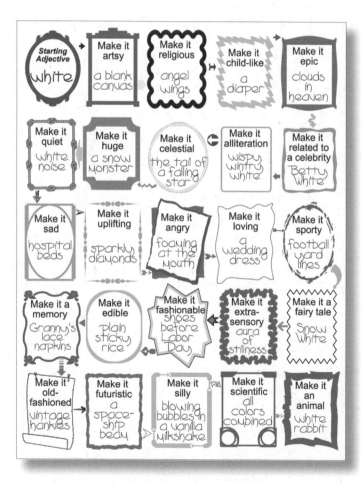

Sample Metaphor Machine

Now, try it yourself using any word you like. You might try using the word *timeless* to start:

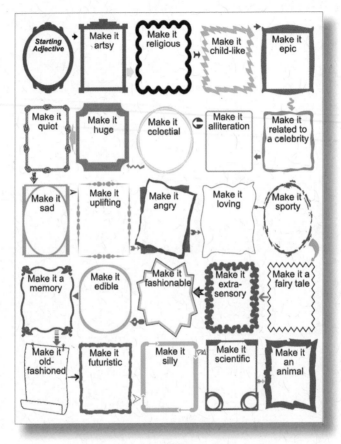

Blank Metaphor Machine

The more you play with metaphor tools like these, the more readily and easily you will find yourself thinking in metaphorical terms on all subjects, including time.

METAPHORS AS HEALERS AND HELPERS

Metaphors are more than just poetic descriptions of things. They can become powerful guides for living and can serve as very helpful tools for rethinking the way we view and experience time. Whenever you are frustrated or stressed about time, you can choose to play with the metaphors to help you see time in a new way. Try this: start by comparing time with another noun, and allow yourself to muse over the implications of the comparison. For example:

- What if, right now, time were an ocean? (How could I better ride out this situation, or appreciate its hidden power, or use its flowing nature?)
- What if time were a newborn? (How could I better nurture it, or how could I appreciate the wisdom of its yet-unspoken words, or what could I learn from its pure heart?)
- What if time were a camera? (As Angela Byers says in the art shown below, "Living my life as a camera means that I get to capture each precious snapshot in my life. It also means that I can quickly erase all of the things that aren't framed just right.")

Digital collage

Living My Life as a Camera by Angela Byers

Mikell's Story: Time as a River

Mixed media collage on board, 18 x 18 in.

River Metaphor by
Mikell Y. Worley

"I recently lost my home and all material possessions in the force of a flood. One might think that I would see a flood as water's most powerful form. But actually, I see *more* power in the peaceful, nurturing, gently flowing river stream that provides nourishment, a home, and recreational opportunities. Seeing time like a river means I have direction and purpose. I can provide nourishment and support to others, carry them along with me and lift them up! I am constantly moving, embracing change, discovering new opportunities around every bend. I can be peaceful without being motionless. At times I can come out of my banks, but I will return to find focus and direction. I can adapt to circumstances by changing form. Time is also gentle, free flowing, and always moving forward. It continuously and eternally flows into — and out of — our lives. My collage of torn, handpainted papers reminds me that if I have difficult times, I will shift my perception, keep moving, and have faith that each bend in the river is taking me where I need to be."   — Mikell Y. Worley

Now, look at time through the lens of an adjective, and again explore new insights. For example:

- What if time were purple? (How would it make me feel? What new possibilities would emerge?)
- What if time were chatty? (What would it tell me? What would I tell it?)

Whenever you're faced with *any* challenge, try opening up the situation to see what lessons are hiding in metaphors. A "bad time" can go through a metamorphosis and often be seen in a whole new light as metaphorical musings add new colors, textures, and depth to the situation.

ARTsignment: Metaphor-morphosis

This process helps you to identify and illustrate a guiding metaphor for your life, which can then inform and inspire new thoughts about time.

Step 1: Answer the journal questions below to identify a metaphor, simile, or analogy to represent your life.

1. Make a list of words that describe how you would most like to feel every day.

2. Select *one word* from your list that seems to most accurately and specifically describe your desired state of being. What objects, ideas, and images relate to this word? For example, if your word is *calm*, then perhaps some images associated with this word might include clouds, a sleeping baby, waterfalls, a still ocean.

3. What images, places, ideas, and things consistently seem to move you and hit you on an emotional level? For each item, write a list of words that describe it.

4. If you could live your life as something nonhuman (such as an animal, a color, or an inanimate object), what would you choose? Why? Write a list of words that describe your choice.

5. Go through all the above responses, and create a short list of a few images that seem to be, symbolically, most connected to *how you want to live your life*.

6. For each item on the new short list, complete this sentence by filling in the blanks with the first words that come to mind. Living my life like _____ means _____. And it means _____. And also it means _____. For example:

Living my life like I'm painting means I don't stress about having enough colors, I just use all the beauty I have. And it means that if something bad happens, I just go with the flow, I just take the new spill and go outside the lines and work to keep creating. And also it means I have some idea of what I want before it starts, but it could turn out being something totally different. And it also means that I get to create it, I get the choices, I decide which colors and brushes to use.

7. Select one metaphor that seems to resonate the most strongly with how you want to live your life. Create a sentence to describe it, such as, "I paint my life with bright colors." This is your new metaphor-mantra.

Step 2: Create a piece of art, using any media or techniques, to represent this metaphor for your life. As you work on your piece of art, contemplate how this metaphor affects your thoughts and perception of time. Let your mind wander far and wide; keeping your hands busy while your mind is moving is a wonderful way to open up all kinds of creative thinking.

For example, if your metaphor is to live life as if you are painting, here are a few ways you might relate that metaphor to your sense of time:

- *I'll never know how time will work out in the end, so why worry? After all, how boring it would be if we knew how the paintings would look in the end; why would we paint them, even?*
- *If I have a bad time, I can just see it as a new color to add new texture and depth to my life.*
- *I won't run out of time and ways to use it, just like I won't run out of color combinations.*

Step 3: How can you integrate this new understanding of both life and time into your day-to-day routine? What do you most want to remember about this exercise? Jot down a few main ideas so that you can hold on to the driving elements of this exercise. Then display your artwork where you can see it often, to reflect on this new guiding metaphor in your life.

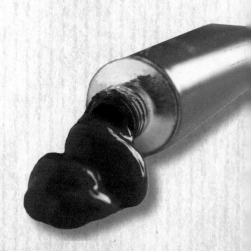

ARTsignment Gallery: Metaphor-morphosis

Digital collage

"Cherry blossoms are such a wonderful symbol for not only the changing of the seasons but the changes in *all* of life. Blooming at the very end of winter, with blossoms that last only a very short while, they are at once both a symbol of hope and a reminder of the fleeting, ever-changing nature of life itself. This impermanence of time is, I think, one of the reasons why we create art. When we create, we leave parts of ourselves on the page where they can bloom forever. This metaphor and artwork remind me simultaneously of the renewal and the impermanence that we find in time."

— MARNEY K. MAKRIDAKIS

ARTsignment Gallery: Metaphor-morphosis

Mixed media on paper, 11 x 14 in.

"As I contemplated the sun as a metaphor for my life and my relationship to time, I felt a willingness to expand my own ray of light and to surrender and trust in the nurturing and supportive aspects of life lived not by the clock but by sunshine time. One of my biggest challenges with time is feeling like there is not enough of it to accomplish my great vision. Through this exercise I found that I can be more like the sun: I need not worry that there is enough time; I can rest when it is time to rest and rise again and continue my journey the next day. Through this process I am taking away a sense of renewal. By changing my perspective and thinking like the sun, I can become more vibrant, confident, alive, and empowered. The future is bright!"

— CHRISTINE DEJULIIS

ARTsignment Gallery: Metaphor-morphosis

Pen and ink on paper, 8.5 x 12 in.

"It took a while, but I finally realized that I can relate to life and time like water. Sometimes I will be free flowing, flooding, tumbling, trickling, resting in quiet solitude, or free falling, and still I can choose to follow the path of least resistance. Every movement is a part of the same thing. Time and water are both renewable resources; it is only I who make them scarce. I created a Zentangle (a meditative, pattern-based art form), and it was a very slow, peaceful exercise with a lot of contemplation. This exercise actually *physically slowed* my life to a different pace as well. Through this project, my energy flow has changed, and I am very much more aware of myself, my thoughts, my feelings, and how I move through life." — LUCINDA POLLIT

ARTsignment Gallery: Metaphor-morphosis

Acrylic on board, 5.75 x 7.75 in.

"My metaphor-mantra is: my life is a colorful, reliable sunset. I painted a sunset using art board and paints I've also had forever but rarely used. I applied about nine different colors and kept smearing them around. This whole 'Let's see what happens' approach is not usually how I roll, and sunsets are very hard to control! But in doing this, I realized that there's no such thing as perfection for a sunset. Sunsets are reliable but not predictable. I remember, when on vacation in Maui, how we wondered if the clouds would clear off 'in time' or if we could get down to the beach 'in time.' The sun still set; there is no 'in time.' You can't force or plan where sunsets are concerned. Simply doing this art and letting my mind wander helped me believe that I can let go of some of the perfection and plans, and still be reliable and beautiful."

— TRISHA MARCY

11. CREATING TIME THROUGH NEW MEASURES

Life in a Day

Poetic Pause

Time as recycling
Empty jars find their purpose
What is left behind?

Webster's dictionary defines *timing* as "the ability to select the precise moment for doing something for optimum effect." When we think of timing, we think of the choices we make and the humble ways in which we are able to control time. Some examples:

- A couple determines the best timing to conceive a child.
- A star quarterback must have excellent timing to pass the football.
- A writer decides when to insert paragraph breaks, to affect the flow of and timing in which her reader absorbs the material.

Of course, in all the examples above, we don't have full control of the results. The act of choosing timing is one of limited, yet valuable, power.

It's an interesting exercise to imagine how different our lives could be with just slight alterations in timing. In the film *Sliding Doors*, we follow two story lines, with the only difference being that the main character catches the train in one story and misses it in the other. What follows are two different narratives, and the viewer is forced to examine how even the smallest changes in timing can change so many details that follow.

We may not be able to see the alternate narratives potentially triggered by our conscious and unconscious choices. But what if we can change what *timing* means in our lives?

FRAGMENTED TIME

One of the problems with our linear perception of time is that we partition it into small fragmented pieces: minutes, hours, days, weeks, months, and so on. By fragmenting time in this way, we can easily forget that there is more to time beyond these divisions. We have to take a trip in three months, and so we worry about that now. We have an assignment due in four days, and so it weighs on our time today. During our habitual yet seemingly randomly selected seven-day week, we wait for the weekend and then dread the upcoming Monday. Our segmentation of days leads to the devaluation of the present moment. Viewing time in this way, we often allow the worries and pressures from the future to reverberate today, like guitar strings humming in a somber key.

> *"I can treat anything in my life as art, including time."*
>
> — BHEKI NAYLOR,
> ARTbundance Coach

It's a crime when we allow life to become a series of meaningless days, marred by pressure, overwhelm, and worry. Whether we're having a "good" day or a "bad" day, in the big picture, *every moment* is equally precious and pregnant with great potential. We must remember that today is just as valuable as that always-distant day in the future when, we are hoping, everything will finally be easier or better.

There's another issue with seeing our time as an endless string of days: it inevitably leads to procrastination. From the little things we can do to take care of our own life to the big things we can do to make a difference in others' lives, it becomes all too easy to put things off and say we will do them "one day." We figure that if we don't take action here or if we put off something there, it's not a problem because there's always "more time."

On the one hand, there is much truth to this; time, at least some variant of it, is eternal, especially when we take an active role in creating time in our own design.

However, if we are to make the most of our time here and now on earth, this linear view of time can be misleading, since we take for granted the opportunities in front of us right now to make meaningful, lasting actions and *live eternally* right now.

EXPERIMENTAL MEASURES

Throughout this book, we have been looking at expanding our experience of time by exploring *qualitative* measurements of time rather than using the traditional quantitative methods of accounting for time, In this chapter, we return to quantitative measurements; they just happen to be different from the ones traditionally used. We will use *new quantitative measurements* to explore changing the timing of, and the timing in, our life.

Great freedom comes when we measure time in quantitative increments beyond the usual minutes and hours. For example, I love measuring my exercise workouts

Acrylic on canvas, 17 x 11 in.

Time as I Want to See It by Gwyn Malloy

by the number of songs that played rather than the number of minutes. This allows me to get lost in the music and the moment, and to get my mind off the clock. My son's bedtime ritual is for me to read him four or five books, depending on when he starts yawning and I feel his weight sink into my lap in sleepy heaviness. "Four or five books" is a quantitative measurement, yet it is a much more natural way to approach bedtime than to have a set time limit, such as "read for fifteen minutes."

Mixed media on canvas, 14 x 11 in.

Time's Yellow Tape Can Never Measure Your Colors
by Marney K. Makridakis

As we've discussed, the real problem with time is perception, as we're always thinking that time is going by too fast or too slow. We can use the enigma of perception to explore time more fully — to travel its dimensions and measure it in different ways. Since we define time by its boundaries, what happens if those boundaries are altered? For example, the moon on the horizon appears larger or smaller based on our perception of it, relative to its surroundings. When it's closer to the horizon, it looks bigger, and when it's alone in the sky, it looks smaller. This perception is created by the *boundaries* around the object. Similarly, we can alter the *boundaries that we place in time* to experiment with a new sense of timing.

For example, what if a "day" were measured every twenty-four minutes rather than twenty-four hours? In this hypothetical scenario, our actual, physical time doesn't change; the only thing that changes is the way we label our days. In this scenario, every one of our regular twenty-four-hour days would then be played out as sixty days, lasting twenty-four minutes each. Take a moment and think about it: how would this affect your life and your sense of time?

When I posed this scenario to a few friends, I received several different responses. Paula Swenson said, "My first thought is that I wouldn't have to try so hard to get so much done every day!" Bradley Harding said, "It seems that life, at least the external, day-to-day experience, would probably function on a completely different level. I think my internal, creative processes would remain the same, but the 'time' it would take to complete a project would be several days, weeks, or months — as opposed to several hours. Many of my peers would not be thrilled with that form of measurement at all!" Karen Karsten enjoyed musing on the implications:

Watercolor on paper, 6 x 3 in.

Clock Crop by Jill Badonsky

The idea of a day being twenty-four minutes seems confining and liberating at the same moment. It's confining since the divisions of the day are broken into so many short pieces, so it feels like things would have to be moving very fast. But it's also liberating because you wouldn't have to wait so long for tomorrow. A new day would be starting soon, with all the things a new day brings. Deciding what a "day" means in terms of usual functions would be so different: no more three meals a day, and you wouldn't even have to sleep every day! I doubt that the bank and stores would open and close sixty times in one cycle of the sun, so maybe things would just be open all the time? My real question is wondering how many birthdays I'd get!

On the other extreme, let's experiment with viewing our entire life as *one single day*. How would things be different if your whole life took place in just one day? I was visiting a planetarium with my family recently and saw a display that truly moved me. It was a visual timeline of the universe, presented as if the entire life of the universe were contained in a single year. Amazingly, from this yearlong perspective, all of human life appears only in the very last final few *minutes*! That's quite a thing to get one's head around: the entirety of human life is held in the tiniest fraction of time, related to what existed before.

I have continued to think of this image, as it is a wonderful reminder of perspective on the grandest scale. It also helped me to realize that we can do something similar with our own lives. What if we could change the timeline of *our* lives so that everything took place within *just one day*? Might this change in perspective be a way to counter some of our patterns of taking time for granted? We all have a long list of things that we say we'll do "one day." How about making your "one day" *right now*? When my student Lori Danyluk tried to imagine this concept, she told me, "If I think about the things we *do*, then the concept of living life in one day is almost impossible for me to get a grasp on. But if I look at who I want to *be*, it has me thinking about the *who I am being* while living it, regardless of what I am doing, so as to make the very most of it." The following ARTsignment guides you to explore time through this new sense of figurative measurement.

ARTSIGNMENT: ONE DAY LIFE/TIME

In this ARTsignment, you'll be *reimagining your life within one single day*. Note that in this exploration, the new quantitative measurement is a figurative one, not a literal one. In other words, the actual length of time lived doesn't change. What *does* change is the label of measurement placed upon that time. Your life is just as long, but it is not segmented into "days."

Step 1: Answer the journal questions below to investigate the concept of reimagining your life within one single day.

1. Think of a recent "bad day" and a recent "good day." Describe the ways in which they are equally valuable and equally meaningful.

2. Does worrying about the past or future cloud your present? Why or why not?

3. If your whole life were just as long in length, but in measurement it was only one day, how might that change your perspective?

4. Describe what you would like your one day to be like. What are you most eager to discover? How do you most want to spend your time? What are you doing? How are you feeling? With whom are you spending time?

5. Describe your one day in more metaphorical terms. What *color* is your one day? What *scent* is your one day? What does your one day *taste* like? If your one day could be symbolized by an inanimate object, what would it be?

6. Make a list of the things you tend to say you'll do "one day." Allow your list to include your big, far-reaching dreams, all the way down to the small things you do to make a difference in your own life and the lives of others.

7. For each item on your list, ask yourself, how might I implement this idea in my life in my "one day"…today?

Step 2: Create a piece of artwork to illustrate your One Day Life/Time, depicting the new perspective of *your life lived in one single day*. You can use any media or techniques that you like. Remember that in this figurative exploration, the actual length of time lived doesn't change. The only thing that changes is the *label* of measurement placed upon that time. Your life is just as long, but it is not segmented into days.

167

Step 3: As you work to create your piece, reflect on how your sense of time morphs in this hypothetical scenario. What happens to time when you don't break it down into tiny segments? How does this affect elements like awareness, appreciation, and procrastination?

Step 4: When your piece is complete, reflect on what you have taken away from these experimental measures. In what way does this exercise influence your sense of time now, back in your regular twenty-four-hour days? What do you want to remember about your One Day Life/Time experience? Place your artwork in a prominent place to help you recall these awarenesses.

ARTsignment Gallery: One Day Life/Time

Mixed media on foam board, 20 x 24 in.

"Once you break away from the firmly rooted industrial, linear idea of time, there are all sorts of possibilities. I thought about time as one long day, without the tick-tock of daily deadlines, no more waiting for the weekend to come around, no saving the best stuff for tomorrow. No anxiety over being late or having the day end in twenty-four hours. I began to think that if we always lived in the *present*, if we put away the past and future, it might be like one long day. What if we didn't parse time into smaller and smaller little sections? These days we can even measure time in nanoseconds, and it seems like everything has to be faster and faster. What if it all stretched out? When I think about time as one day, I think of it like a lake, with connections to the earth and the universe. There's total joy in diving into the lake: no waiting for the weekend here! I felt like this ARTsignment offered a little key to unlocking time. Come with me to this lake, swim in the stardust, surf with the music of time, unlock time for yourself." — KAREN KARSTEN

ARTsignment Gallery: One Day Life/Time

Collaged book cover, 3 x 3 in.

Front

Sample interior spreads

"For my One Day Life/Time, I decorated a small cardboard book, with each spread illustrating something that I tend to put off for 'one day.' The book serves as a reminder for the changes that I can make right now, simply by not taking time for granted. I used vintage advertisements to illustrate the concepts I wanted to convey, further adding to the idea that self-care is timeless. The simplicity of the images allows me to really focus on the words, and let these important reminders sink in. I can refer to it any time I need a gentle reminder that time, no matter how it's sliced, is all about *now*."
— MARNEY K. MAKRIDAKIS

ARTsignment Gallery: One Day Life/Time

Acrylic on board, 6 x 8 in.

"Today is the day that I time-lapse my life. It is a warm and sunny day, and I feel happy. I am present, and I inhale the essence of *me* deep to my soul today. I am humming the music of my life, as I rejoice in the love that surrounds me and know that my heart is full. Today, I have realized that I am a survivor, I am a dreamer, I am a lover of life. I am a mother, a sister, a daughter, and a friend. I know that the tears I cry wash away the sorrow and that I must allow the ebb and flow both to have their time in order to feel balanced. In this, my one day, I am reminded to look for the laughter, for the love that presents itself to me. Seeing my life in this way — as one day — reminds me that all the moments, minutes, and hours of my life, both good and bad, have made me the person that I am today. I realize that I would not change a single thing, but I will now be more present for the moments here and now and appreciate this marvelous life of mine."

— PATRICIA J. MOSCA

ARTsignment Gallery: One Day Life/Time

Colored pencil on paper, 13.25 x 11 in.

"My piece is titled *One Minute to Midnight*. In my one-day life, I am the sphinx moth just shed of cocoon. My wings stiffen and strengthen as they dry, and I'm eager to be off experiencing my day. I buzz as powerfully as a hummingbird. My tongue finds honeysuckle, which I return to again and again. The nectar is the sustainer of my life and this day. The scent of honeysuckle drives me to nectaring, powering me. Cool morning turns to warm afternoon, cooling once again at dusk. As the day draws to a close, I sense the urge to procreate. I must prepare the way for who will follow me the next day. A joyous mating, eggs are secreted, and as my energy drains, I float away on the breeze. I am wild, free, and completely unaware of my one-day mortality. Choice is mine. The most important thing I took away from this ARTsignment was the absolute of presence. BEing in every single moment."

— NANLEAH N. MICK

12. CREATING TIME THROUGH SYNCHRONICITY

Time beside Time

Poetic Pause

Time as the white moon
You and I see the same one
Coinciding dreams

When we embrace nonlinear time, we can explore *synchronicity* as a new way to order our personal time. Synchronicity refers to the awareness of meaningful connections between objects, people, events, symbols, and feelings. The word literally means "same time"; Carl Jung coined it to describe what he called "an acausal connecting principle" that links mind and matter. He identified three types of synchronicity:

1. The coinciding of a thought or feeling with an outside event
2. A dream, a vision, or a premonition of something that happens in the future
3. A dream or vision that coincides with an event occurring at a distance

Scientific fields of quantum physics, fractal geometry, and chaos theory provide a context for synchronicity, as many scientists believe that all components of life, from people and animals to cells and molecules, are part of an all-encompassing web of information and that no event is ever isolated unto itself. In my own "web of life," I've noticed that synchronicity reveals itself in both ordinary and extraordinary circumstances. Examples include, but are not limited to, premonitions about events and ideas, surprising connections with other people, meaningful associations taken on by objects and symbols, and inspired ideas and plans that seem to "match up" with external experiences.

SYNCHRONICITY AND TIME

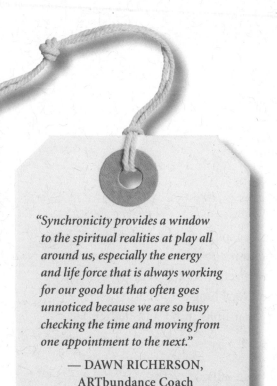

"*Synchronicity provides a window to the spiritual realities at play all around us, especially the energy and life force that is always working for our good but that often goes unnoticed because we are so busy checking the time and moving from one appointment to the next.*"

— DAWN RICHERSON,
ARTbundance Coach

Observing synchronicity allows us to *get out of sequential time* and invite a sense of enchantment and new possibility into our lives. By their very nature, synchronicities involve patterns that transcend the usual limits of space and time. They provide a glimpse of something beyond our normal rationality and our general understanding of how space and time work. Curiosity about how the world works is inherent in all of us, regardless of culture or religious background. Nurturing our curiosity stimulates both our creativity and our humanity.

Synchronicity awakens and expands our natural curiosity with new examinations of what we believe, what we don't believe, and what we *might* believe. Stretching our belief muscles in this way spills over into stretching our perception of time and how time works. When we can grasp the possibility that the connective space-time threads in synchronicity are a *natural flowing of time*, then we see synchronicity no longer as events but simply as a way to experience space-time itself.

Perhaps synchronicity is more ordered than we think it is. Perhaps synchronicity *is* a more natural ordering of time, but it seems rare to us because our experience of time is fragmented. Perhaps the more present, connected, and aware we are, the more we see that synchronicity is the norm and not the exception.

SYNCHRONICITY AND MEANING

People often wonder what a synchronistic event means in the big picture of their lives. You check the clock and it's 4:44, and you realize that you have been checking the clock at 4:44 all week. You have a dream about a gerbil and then your child brings one home from school. You think of an old friend you haven't thought of in a long time and then get an email from him. Do these space-time collisions mean anything?

When something synchronistic happens, to me it means that I'm aware and open and seeing connections that are nonlinear, nonsequential, and nonchronological. I also interpret it as a signal that I'm on the right track, somehow; the energy of life is communicating with me, and I'm listening.

When something synchronistic happens to me, I stop and take a moment to see if there is something further that I want to pursue related to the situation. Synchronistic events are wonderful signposts for decisions to make or directions to follow. To use an example from modern technology, a synchronistic event is like an alarm that goes off in my phone, reminding me to make a phone call to my intuition. I call my intuition to say hello and check in, and I see if there is anything else I need to know or an action I might take that is inspired by the situation. If I hadn't heard synchronicity's "alarm," I would have missed this opportunity to check in.

As this example underlines, I believe that synchronicity's meaning is entirely

Leslie's Story: Synchronicity Is Everywhere

"I no longer see anything in life as coincidental. I've come to embrace synchronicity completely, seeing it everywhere, in both the marvelous and the mundane. This is life; this is the fragmented plane that is not really fragmented at all. Every day, every moment contains synchronicity, and I can look back to the beginning of my memories and know this. The time in the park when a stranger held me in his arms as I sobbed, then let me go without an agenda. The time when I spoke with a debt counselor who made calls and set into motion a variety of things to begin decreasing my debt, and then a truck T-boned my car in an intersection that same afternoon, and the insurance payout allowed me to pay off several bills and breathe more easily. The time when I tripped and fell on the sidewalk, and a woman in the class I was teaching and a strong young man were right there to help me back up. My mind is so full of synchronicity that it has become blank in terms of synchronistic events, mainly because I believe I am always living within synchronicity, so events don't separate themselves."
— Leslie Dupont

subjective; it's about me and what I personally take from the experience rather than an objective analysis of the experience and its potential value. This means that both ordinary and extraordinary synchronicities can be equally full of potential meaning.

I was recently reading Robert Grudin's book *Time and the Art of Living*, in which he says, "Our common image of experience is about as accurate as a still photograph of a man riding a bicycle. Project this image back into reality, and the man will fall off his bicycle." Less than half an hour later, I quite randomly stumbled on a photograph of a bicyclist in my own collection of vintage photos. It was an ordinary convergence of coincidental moments, but one that I couldn't help noticing. So I looked for the message or lesson that might be hidden in the odd little convergence of time and space. I went back to reread the quote from the book, now taking my time to fully absorb it.

As I revisited the words, I realized that they were just what I needed to jostle my current resistance to change and embrace change itself as a comforting constant. The few months prior to this event had been marked by change and motion. I had felt an almost desperate longing for stillness, yet the serendipitous pairing of Grudin's quote and the photograph that I found moments later reminded me that although we can have moments of stillness, life itself is *always* moving, in constant momentum. I am so thankful for this convergence of coincidental moments because it brought my attention to exactly where it needed to be. In fact, I created a piece of art around the photo of the man on the bicycle, and I keep it on my desk to connect me back to that coinciding moment in time, when a photo and a quote converged to bring me a powerful life lesson.

Thoughts on Synchronicity
by Marilyn Harris Mills

Mixed media journal page, 7 x 7 in.

Digital collage

"Our common image of experience is about as accurate as a man riding a bicycle."

- Robert Grudin

Life moves forward.
Change is constant.

Synchronous Message by Marney K. Makridakis

Synchronistic events can be simple, ordinary experiences, like connecting a quote with a photograph. Or they can be extraordinary circumstances that don't even seem believable. When I was in college, I woke up one morning with a strong urge to attend a church down the street from my apartment. I did not regularly attend church, so the pull seemed rather random. In fact, I didn't even know what kind of church it was or anything about it at all. Yet the intuitive hunch was so strong that I just couldn't shake it, so finally I thought I'd just take a walk there, at the very least. I did in fact enter, and I sat down in a pew to attend the service. I was stunned when the minister began his sermon by reading a quote from Carlyle Marney, who was my father's mentor, the man for whom I was named!

I was beaming the whole time and filled with a sense of wonder; in fact, during the hymns, I must have been singing extra-loudly because after the service, the gentleman sitting next to me in the pew complimented me on my "joyful singing." We introduced ourselves, and when he heard my last name, his eyes widened. It turned out that he and my father had been in the same study group of young philosophers

Terry's Story: Riding Synchronicity's Waves

"Synchronicity plays a huge role in my life. It appears so much that I cannot escape noticing, and yet I still feel childlike in my absolute joy of recognizing it, almost as though it is magic. I think of the synchronicities as markers, guideposts, reminders that all is well. Each time I notice this happen, I smile inside my heart and say 'thank you' to all the helpers I sense within and around me. It makes me feel as though the Universe is a safe place. It feels magical and light, joyous and playful, just plain fun.

"When I think of synchronicity in my life, I think of an experience I had years ago, when my husband, Bob, and I were in a white-water canoe race. We had never canoed together, and now we were about to race in white water! The river was rated a grade IV because of the high waves, rocks, sharp turns, steep drop-offs. We capsized within thirty seconds of the gun. Suddenly we were under water, flailing around. Bob threw his paddle away to try to swim, and I was digging my feet into the rocks to try to stop from moving so fast in the rapids. We finally made it to shore, righted the canoe, found the other paddle, and got back in and back into the race. Within another twenty minutes, we hit another section of white water and capsized again. This time we had some struggles, but we were able to right ourselves quickly. By the time we capsized the third time, it was so easy to just enjoy the feel of the water, notice where the rocks were, and guide ourselves easily around them and literally 'go with the flow.' It was actually fun, and we were able to

continued on next page

in the sixties — a group that had met halfway across the country and been led by…none other than Carlyle Marney! Hearing the quote in the sermon, he was reflecting on his old colleagues, including my father, with whom he had not connected in many years, and there I was, sitting right next to him!

What I find interesting about these two examples is that the "ordinary" experience had as much of an impact on me as the "extraordinary" experience, if not more. A synchronous event doesn't need to be epic and theatrical; it can be very simple. As with everything in life — and, for that matter, everything in time — it's all about our *perception* rather than the event itself.

CULTIVATING SYNCHRONICITY

Becoming more aware of synchronicity is a wonderful creative skill to cultivate. A synchronistic experience, regardless of *why* you believe it happens, is a unique opportunity to get outside your normal space-time trajectory and see information in a new light. Experiencing synchronicity requires a certain change in linear time; we must slow down the way we are metabolizing time, because so often synchronicity appears in little things that you would never even notice if you were hurrying. Just as our personal experiences become more meaningful and memorable when we "stop them in time" by recording them in journals, letters, emails, and even conversations, keeping a *synchronicity log or journal* helps keep synchronicity alive in our consciousness as a present force, as a new *order of time*.

I've kept a synchronicity log on and off for years, and I find that when I'm not actively recording synchronicities, I don't see them nearly as often. Naturally, this is supreme evidence for those who believe that synchronicity is exclusively the result of chance and desire. Indeed it is true: whenever we actively seek anything, we see it *more*, and we can use this psychological phenomenon to our benefit. If you're looking for things to be grateful for, you're going to see more ways to be grateful. If you're looking for wonderful

continued from previous page

right ourselves when the time was perfect, not struggle against the current or debris in the river.

"My perception of noticing the synchronicities in my life is like the third time after capsizing: so fun, just going with the flow of life and truly able to be guided, as well as make gentle decisions: which way to go, when to get back in the boat, when to just flow with the river of life. I don't want to slow the synchronicities down, necessarily; I slow *myself* down so that I can appreciate them.

"The flow is strong, like a class IV or V river, but I am in complete, relaxed control, just riding the waves, gliding over the rocks, missing the branches altogether, and noticing the sights along the way, filled with wonder and gratitude."   — Terry Jordan

ways to spend your time, you'll find more wonderful ways to spend your time. If you're having a bad day and you just keep seeing things that are going wrong, you get more of the same. Similarly, as we become more intent on looking for synchronicity and its accompanying guidance, we will see more of it.

Shelley Lindsey, one of my students, had several insights when she began to track synchronicity in her life: "As I started writing down the things that are happening, I saw how many times the 'Red Sea' has parted. It makes me aware of times when I have paid attention and followed the cleared path, and other times when I just stood there, and drowned. Keeping a written log of synchronicity made me pay attention to the power of positive thinking, how *looking for what I need* brings it to me."

TRACKING SYNCHRONICITY

When I'm actively tracking synchronicity, I like to follow a particular structure each morning and evening to provide continuity to my journal entries. In the morning, I jot down several key elements:

- Dreams
- Hunches
- Random ideas in the form of *synchronotes*, my made-up word for things that you notice are dancing on your brain; these things may turn out to have significance as you continue to cultivate a synchronicity habit
- Intention for the day

In the evening, I review what I wrote that morning and reflect on any new meanings, patterns, or connections that have emerged.

Here is a simple structure you can follow for the morning entries:

1. **Dreams:** Were there any meaningful elements in last night's dream?
2. **Hunches:** Do you have any hunches for today — just feelings about actions you should take or things you might do?
3. **Synchronotes catching my eye:** Jot down a few synchronotes. Write the first thing you think of for each of the following prompts. If nothing comes to mind, you can just make something up.

   An image:
   Something that catches your eye in your immediate environment:
   A person:
   A place:
   A smell:
   Anything else that is dancing in your mind:

4. **Intention:** Write down your intention for the day.

Here is a simple structure for the evening entries:

1. **Intention:** Review your intention for the day and make notes about its role in your day.
2. **Connections:** Review your synchronotes from this morning and explore any connections between your notes and your day. Did any of the images or thoughts from your synchronotes find their way into your life today?

3. **Hunches:** Any hunches that you followed up on today? Any hunches that you haven't followed up on?

4. **Shifts:** Are you noticing any change in the clarity or frequency of synchronicity? Are you noticing any change in your overall feeling, mood, energy, perception?

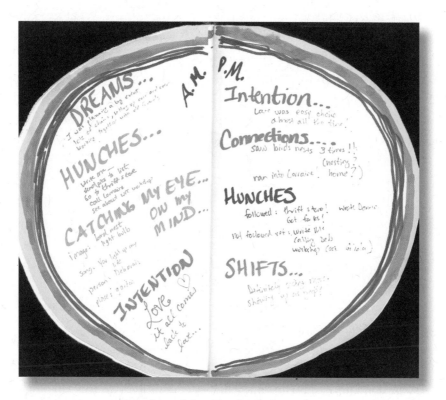

Synchronicity Tracking Sample

How you decide to track synchronicity is a personal choice, and your tracking method can be so much more meaningful when you personalize it so that it is connected to you and your own sense of life and time. The ARTsignment that follows invites you to create a personalized synchronicity tracking method to support your new awareness in this area. Through synchronicity, we move from a life lived "time after time" to one lived "time beside time," expanding the breadth of time and the way we experience it.

ARTsignment: Synchronicity Watch

Like anything else, looking for synchronicity increases our chances to see it. Keeping track of synchronicity and other messages from your intuition is a wonderful habit. This project guides you to create a Synchronicity Watch: a tool to help you become more aware of synchronicity in your life.

Step 1: Think about the role of synchronicity in your life. What does that word mean to you? Another term for synchronicity is *coincidence*; what events have "coincided" with one another in your life to bring you where you are today?

Step 2: Plan a design for your Synchronicity Watch: a tracking system you can use to watch synchronicity at play in your life. You may want to create a new journal or notebook, or perhaps collect your thoughts in a special box or other receptacle.

Step 3: As you create your Synchronicity Watch, allow your mind to open up to perceive synchronicity in new ways. Try writing a *synchronicity mantra*: a phrase that affirms your intentions that you can repeat over and over. Some examples:

> *As the symbols of my life become more and more meaningful to me, my life becomes more joyful and fulfilling.*
>
> *More and more, I see the purposes behind every single thing that happens to me.*
>
> *My hunches are becoming more and more clear to me, and are constantly leading me to meaningful events.*
>
> *I receive helpful information from the perfect sources.*

Terry Jordan and Leslie Dupont, whose stories appear in this chapter, phrased their affirmations this way, respectively: "Each time I notice a symbol, I know and trust that I am just where I need to be. I am divinely guided in each and every moment" and "I am present within and always a part of an infinite web of connection."

If you like, you can incorporate your mantra into your Synchronicity Watch.

Step 4: After you complete your Synchronicity Watch, write your first entry. You can use the structure suggested in the "Tracking Synchronicity" section above, or create your own format.

Step 5: Continue to make entries in your Synchronicity Watch regularly. You'll probably see the biggest changes if you make a brief entry each morning and each night, but you can also try different configurations to see how this playful activity can best fit in your life.

ARTsignment Gallery: Synchronicity Watch

Mixed media assemblage, 2.5 x 9.5 x 1 in.

"Before I began this process, I felt that synchronicity was pretty present and active in my life. However, I didn't have a daily practice of awareness, so I was open to exploring and potentially going even deeper. I knew immediately that I wanted to make a pocket wristwatch. Wearing this fun creative watch keeps this awareness more in the top of my mind. The pocket includes bits of notepaper so I can also write down my synchronicity noticings. Who knows what kinds of synchronicities will be created, from just people being curious about this funky little watch? Wearing the watch has been fun and has helped me to see all the more deeply how connected we are every day, every moment."
— JAN BLOUNT

ARTSIGNMENT GALLERY: SYNCHRONICITY WATCH

Acrylic on paper, 12 x 9 in.

"Rather than starting a separate journal for synchronicity, I am including my synchronistic events in my existing journal, color-coding the entries to make things easy to find. My daily journaling is in pink, my dreams are in blue, and my synchronistic events are highlighted in green because to me the color green means flourishing, growing, and ever changing. I also created a visual reminder to help me pay attention to synchronicity: meet Synchronicity Sam. I enjoy looking at Sam and am filled with delight each time I see him keeping watch for me. Sam is lighthearted and fun although diligent on his watch. His call, 'See it all, see it all, see it all,' is easy for me to remember and a joyful reminder to pay attention. Sam told me that his name stands for 'Seeing All Messages,' and I discovered that the name, being short for Samuel, means 'God has heard' in Hebrew." — SHERYL ALLEN

ARTsignment Gallery: Synchronicity Watch

Mixed media assemblage, 7 x 3.5 in.

"I created a Synchronicity Watch Angel to further open my eyes, heart, and mind to synchronicities at play every day. I began with an angel figurine and adorned her with symbols that are meaningful to me. As I engaged in this ARTsignment, I thought about how I could look at time through a different lens, and so I added the old pair of glasses to my Synchronicity Angel. This experience has me contemplating the intersection of spirituality and time. Moving forward, I want to 'see' the multidimensionality of time and experience its gifts to mind, body, heart, and soul even as I bring myself consciously and more fully to the time that is given to me."

— DAWN RICHERSON

ARTSIGNMENT GALLERY: SYNCHRONICITY WATCH

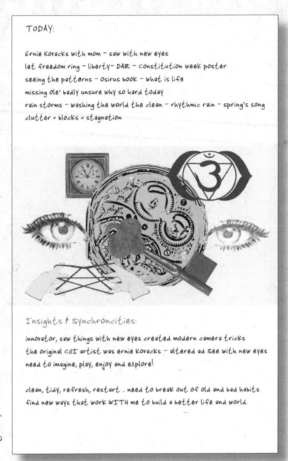

TODAY:

Ernie Kovacks with mom – saw with new eyes
let freedom ring – liberty – DAR – constitution week poster
seeing the patterns – osirus book – what is life
missing Ole' badly unsure why so hard today
rain storms – washing the world the clean – rhythmic rain – spring's song
clutter = blocks = stagnation

Insights & Synchronicities:

innovator, saw things with new eyes created modern camera tricks
the original CGI artist was ernie kovacks – altered ad see with new eyes
need to imagine, play, enjoy and explore!

clean, tidy, refresh, restart .. need to break out of old and bad habits
find new ways that work WITH me to build a better life and world.

Digital journal

"Due to the way synchronicity journals are often laid out, it can be hard to search for things in order to make connections. So I created a digital journal in the form of a writable PDF, which is stored online. I can access it while at work, on my laptop, while traveling, or even on my phone. I would also like to develop a sketch-based watch journal, where I could sketch during the day and then explore if it syncs up with other things that I've noticed. I find that sometimes ideas translate better for me visually than verbally, so it will be interesting to try this experiment with time as well."

— JENNIFER WALLING

13. CREATING TIME THROUGH VISUALIZATION

A Good, Hard Look at "Hard Times"

Poetic Pause

Time as golden leaf
Oblivious to the fall
Embrace winds of change

We have an unfortunate tendency during hard times, whether economic, emotional, or physical, to lose our capacity to take the very actions that will help us the most. Our default mode is often rationalizing that there is "no time" for anything but work and worry. I have come to believe that the exact opposite is true. It is said that necessity is the mother of invention, and so it stands to reason that times when it feels like there is so much necessity are the very moments with the purest potential for true, passionate invention.

Personal challenges affect all dimensions of our life, and certainly time is one of them. One of the benefits of time is that its very passing brings greater meaning to challenges. The farther challenges move from the present into the past, the greater our capacity to see a wider context for their roles in our lives. When I think about the most challenging times in my life, I am able to see how much I learned from those challenges and how the difficulties played a significant role in the overall narrative of my life. The relationship between the clarity of this understanding and the passage of time is a direct one; the more time that passes, the more we seem to see and know. As one of my favorite artists, my friend Terri St. Cloud, expressed,

"Bad times in my life are now gifts that I hold. I look back and see what I got out of them, and know they've added to the now. They've changed and seasoned me and made me who I am today."

A woman named Becky Teter was a significant maternal figure to me for most of my life. When I was growing up, she lived loudly, wildly, and eccentrically in the house across the street, and she lived loudly, inevitably, and indelibly in the hearts of anyone who knew her. In early 2011, Becky passed away after a fight with aggressive ovarian cancer that lasted an unbelievable eight years. Somehow, with each of the hundreds of chemo treatments she received, her faith and will became stronger and stronger. Several years ago, Becky edited a book of essays by ovarian cancer survivors, titled *TORCH: Tales of Remarkable Courage and Hope*. In her preface, Becky said, "Ovarian cancer has marinated me in mercy. I have been tenderized." I love these words of Becky's and reflect on them whenever challenge extends its hand.

This is the beautiful truth of challenge: we all can be "tenderized" if we let the experience seep in. One of the most inspiring movie lines I've ever heard is from the movie *Braveheart*, when Mel Gibson's character, William Wallace, is awaiting certain death and slowly reassures the woman he loves in his delicious Scottish accent that she need not worry for him, since "every man dies...not every man truly *lives*." These words provide a wake-up call, especially when we are in the midst of challenge, to focus on what we are really called to do here on earth, which is not just to be born and die but to truly be alive, as Becky did until her very last breath.

It is the *challenges* in our life that provide us with the richest opportunities to come alive, and to be alive ultimately means *to be moving in time*. We can meet our challenging times with fierce courage and sometimes even fierce silliness and joy, as we face them with a truly brave heart and a child's spirit of wonder. We can boldly meet our hard times head-on and walk away from them even more alive, ever more *vivid in time*.

CHALLENGES IN PAST, PRESENT, AND FUTURE

The way we label our challenges often includes a time element; we use phrases like *hard time*, *challenging time*, and *rough time* to describe them. Whether they are big

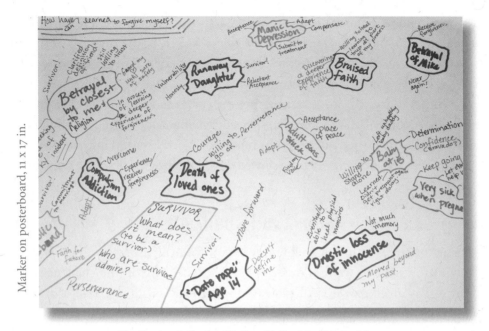

Marker on posterboard, 11 x 17 in.

Challenge Mind Map by Kelly Noel Morrison

challenges (such as a life-threatening illness) or small challenges (such as a toilet overflowing), difficult times *affect* time itself. Furthermore, all states of time are somehow jarred by challenges. In the past state, challenges can become increasingly understood, as previously mentioned, but they also can become more distorted, as we add our own subjective context to the circumstances, when imagination mixes with facts to create our memories. We often telescope the timing of circumstances and events, much as a screenwriter does in writing a scene, where the actual amount of time lapsed is condensed to "save time" in the film. We do the same thing in our memories. For example, we forget that the painful event was not a single event but part of a continuum of small, indiscernible actions that took place for months before and afterward. Time does funny things to pain. It *heals*, yes, and also *reels*, as it spins off in its own directions, making its own meanings.

Additionally, challenges affect our view of the future. In fact, the most common manifestations of challenges are the states of worry and anxiety. Interestingly, these states are usually reflections of the *future* rather than the present. Challenge seems to propel our thoughts to the future at lightning speed, while our bodies are still stuck in the present. It's as if our challenges take us into some underground time-traveling device in which we are moving at top speed to someplace we can't imagine, all the while not being able to see where we are. No wonder we worry!

In the present, challenges deeply change our experience of space-time. Callie Carling describes her experience of time since recently receiving a diagnosis of aggressive breast cancer: "I am seesawing between time moving far too quickly and then, at other moments, far too slowly, especially when we are waiting around in hospitals for tests to be carried out or results reported. When I walked into the consultation room to hear the diagnosis, time slowed down yet speeded up at the same time."

TIME AND ENDURANCE

Challenges often result in our feeling out of control in all aspects of our life, especially with time. When we find ourselves face-to-face with all the challenges that happen in any given day, it is all too easy to lose touch with our *choices* and just surrender to having a "bad day" or the all-encompassing "bad time."

We can take back this control by developing the endurance and perseverance that allow us to move through all kinds of times, even challenging times, with grace

Mixed media journal spread, 7 x 14 in.

Calendure Journal by Marilyn Harris Mills

and joy. A great tool to accomplish this is to *energetically plan ahead*. We put a lot of energy into planning our external time (our events and activities), yet we don't put a lot of activity into planning our *internal time* (our energy and outlook).

Approaching challenges through time is like using the aperture of a camera. The aperture is the opening in the lens that is adjusted to allow in a certain amount of light; this determines the image's *depth of field*. It lets you control the focus of what is seen in the background and foreground. For example, if you are photographing a person in front of a house and focus on the person, shooting at a lower aperture number (indicating a larger lens opening) puts the person in sharp focus and the house in soft focus yet still identifiable. If you want the house to be more sharply focused as well, you shoot at a higher aperture number (for a smaller lens opening). This metaphor reminds us that *we can always choose what to focus on*, and we can use the unique attributes of time to help us do that, as we travel through the different dimensions of time to help us experience challenging times in completely new ways.

I once read a suggestion to spend a few moments before sleep visualizing what the next day would be like, in its most positive light. When I began doing this, I noticed a huge shift in how my days carried out. The changes were so pronounced that I simply could not deny them. Just this small, simple act of visualizing the next day's activities going smoothly made all the difference.

I've been experimenting with this method for a while, and I've found that I have far better results when I visualize the *energy* or *essence* that I want to experience rather than visualizing actual activities. In other words, I focus on the way I want to *feel* the next day rather than what I want to be doing. For most people, this is definitely a new kind of planning, and it takes some getting used to, especially with regard to planning for challenging situations.

The very reason why this kind of positive visualization works is the same reason why planning day-to-day activities can often lead to frustration: whether we like it or not, *perception is very closely related to anticipation*. Think of a time when you planned a fantastic activity and then it fell through, leaving you full of disappointment. On the other hand, think of an instance when you were expecting to have a bad time and something wonderful happened, which took you by surprise and thoroughly delighted you. Life is odd and unpredictable, and we can never really know what will happen until after time has passed. Focusing on planning activities and events can lead to disappointment and frustration when the unexpected chaos of life intervenes and things don't go as we had planned. So, instead of focusing on planning *activities*, we can focus on planning for our *personal endurance*, tapping into the *energy* and *essence* of how we want to feel, especially during challenging situations.

Endurance Planning paves the way for us to continue to connect to positive feelings, no matter what happens to our plans. Patience is one of the only ways that we naturally affect the perception of time with simply our will, and endurance is an active extension of patience. When we "hold our patience," we hold on to what matters.

ENDURANCE PLANNING

Collage on chipboard, 8.75 x 6 in.

Calendure by Gerrie Johnnic

Endurance Planning involves an easy bit of time traveling each evening, before you go to sleep. All you need to do is take about five minutes before you fall asleep and vividly imagine yourself going through the next day, focusing on how you want to feel as you move through the activities of the day. As you imagine yourself in tomorrow's day, pay special attention to any challenges you anticipate and the things you'll be doing that you don't necessarily like to do. Visualize yourself gliding through those challenges, holding on to the *feelings* you want.

Woz Flint tried this technique and loved it, explaining, "This helped me look at planning completely differently! I would always try to picture what my perfect day would look like, but that involved the *actions*. I love that this was about the *feeling*. Some of the days didn't look a thing like I thought they physically would, but they *felt* just like I'd hoped."

If you are new to visualization, or if you feel uncomfortable or distracted, try this: imagine that you are looking at a huge movie screen, watching a movie of yourself carrying out tomorrow's activities, and observe yourself feeling the desired feelings. For some, this technique is helpful, as it may be easier to visualize *watching yourself* rather than *being yourself* in the present moment. You might want to try both techniques and see which one you like the best. Play with these ideas in your imagination for about five minutes each night. Then, when you find yourself in the midst of a challenging situation, you can easily tap into your personal endurance by revisiting these images. Whether you use Endurance Planning for tomorrow's day, the coming year, or anything in between, the process of *energetically planning ahead* is a powerful way to create new experiences with time, even in the midst of challenge.

Endurance Planning for a New Year

If we choose to make New Year's resolutions, we often don't make them until January 1 or even after. But in truth, few things in life can succeed without real preparation. By the time most people recover from the holidays and get serious about their goals for the new year, the year is already several days or weeks old, and then they already feel behind in something they haven't even begun. I think people with creative temperaments are especially sensitive to feeling behind, and this feeling only serves to thwart productivity. Even though my creative spirit thrives on being spontaneous and even a bit impetuous, I aim to make my New Year's resolutions early because I find it so very helpful in following through with my intentions.

When you set your intentions early, you can apply the Endurance Planning approach by spending time *imagining* yourself embarking on your resolutions and seeing how everything potentially plays out, as you focus on the feelings you want to feel. After spending some time with these mental dress rehearsals, you can explore both practical and emotional questions, such as the following:

- Are your resolutions realistic?
- Do you notice places where you might need more information or greater support to help you?
- What pitfalls or blocks can you anticipate and identify beforehand, so that you can be more prepared for them?
- Most important, which feelings that you imagined felt the best?
- How might you ground yourself in these feelings as you prepare for the new year?

ARTsignment: Calendure

This ARTsignment invites you to create a Calendure to help you get motivated and keep track of your Endurance Planning. I invite you to try this process for at least five to seven days and see if you notice a significant change in your life and time.

Step 1: Answer the following journal questions to help you home in on how you would most like to feel, especially during challenging situations.

1. How do you *most* want to feel every day? Make a list of several words that describe your desired state of being.
2. How do these words *feel* in your body? For example, if your word is *peaceful*, what does peaceful feel like?
3. What is the biggest challenge in your life right now? How would you like to feel, in relation to that challenge? Again, try to focus in on a couple of words that viscerally describe how you want to feel.
4. How does your body experience those feelings?
5. Think of what you have planned for tomorrow. What are tomorrow's biggest potential challenges?
6. How would you most like to feel during these challenges tomorrow, and what are the sensations in your body that are associated with these feelings?
7. Explore the role of endurance in your life. What challenges have you endured in the past? Make a list of the things that you have been able to endure and challenges that you have been able to overcome. What skills and strengths have you developed in getting through those difficult challenges? What are you most proud of?
8. After reviewing your answers to the previous questions, what *symbols and images* come to mind when you think of your own personal endurance? Select one or more images or symbols that are particularly relevant; you can now incorporate these images into your Calendure.

Step 2: Make a commitment to try Endurance Planning for at least five to seven days straight. This is the kind of thing that works only if you *do* it rather than just think about doing it. If you feel resistance, remind yourself that it's just five minutes a day, and it has the potential to make a big difference in how you experience your time. I hope you will give it a try!

Step 3: Design a Calendure — a method you can use to track your nights of Endurance Planning. Your Calendure serves as a tangible symbol of your commitment to experiment with this new type of planning, and it also provides a motivational tool to help you track that commitment. You can create your Calendure using any format, with any media, art supplies, or techniques that you like. Here are some suggestions to keep in mind:

- Incorporate imagery that symbolizes your own endurance, perseverance, and strength. By using these symbols, you'll automatically be fueling this process with the power of your personal strength!
- Create a way that you can check off each of your nights of Endurance Planning.
- Design something easily replicable or extendable, to make it easy and convenient to use your Calendure as you continue practicing Endurance Planning.

Step 4: Now start your sequence of nights, following the instructions given above for practicing Endurance Planning. Try incorporating the words, feelings, and body

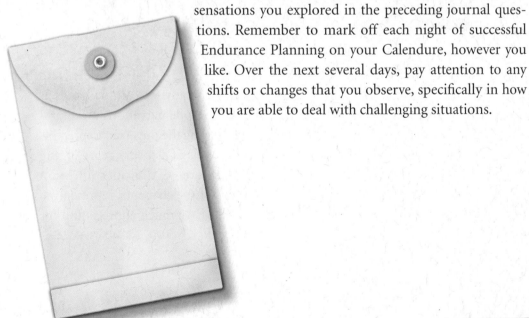

sensations you explored in the preceding journal questions. Remember to mark off each night of successful Endurance Planning on your Calendure, however you like. Over the next several days, pay attention to any shifts or changes that you observe, specifically in how you are able to deal with challenging situations.

Watercolor and colored pencil on paper, 11 x 11 in.

"My Calendure features Alchemystra, my 'Calendure Girl.' Her hair is golden, and the center of the clock is her heart. Alchemystra holds steady, welcoming hands as she extends to each demarcation of the five days. These demarcations are represented by breath marks, a symbol used in music reminding the musician to breathe. The background design of my clock includes the symbols of alchemy, representing my ability to bounce back and make something valuable out of difficult stuff. From breath mark to breath mark, I am using the symbols of the elements, representing my solid ground, fluid motion, interest, and breath. I have much appreciation for this journey."

— CHRIS HAMMER

ARTsignment Gallery: Calendure

Marker on textured paper, 11 x 17 in.

"When I saw the title of this ARTsignment, my mind automatically assumed that this was going to be difficult and maybe not so fun. Through the journal questions, though, I went deeper and explored the differences between a victim, a survivor, and a champion. I realized that I am a champion! I found the Endurance Planning helpful. I try to visualize my way through the steps it will take to complete a task. I often feel heavy. By intentionalizing and visualizing what I want my *energy* to be, I am set free from the heavy feeling, and I approach the task with a lighter heart/mind."

— KELLY NOEL MORRISON

ARTsignment Gallery: Calendure

Mixed media decoupage, 6 x 6 in.

"Every design idea I had for my Calendure included a flower in some way as the means of checking off my nights of Endurance Planning. Some versions included flower petals themselves as the means of tracking each night, but I eventually decided against that, as I wouldn't have liked the looks of the incomplete flower on the first four nights. I decided to go with a little flower garden that would grow up one flower at a time so that even when the little garden wasn't full of flowers, there would be fully developed little flowers to gaze upon. This imagery represents the growth that occurs in big and little ways that aren't even apparent sometimes. Each stage of my personal journey is represented in those little blossoms."

— TAMMY HENSLEY

14. CREATING TIME THROUGH PERMISSION

The Right to Set the Time Right

Poetic Pause

Time as a wrapped gift
Bound, contained, idealized
Ribboned intentions

O ne of my workshop participants, Lanette Breedt, once said, "I think the time is right to set the time right in my own life." It sounds like a tongue twister, but I love the phrase's meaning. It's very empowering to realize that we can *set the time in our life*, and set it right. What might it look like to set the time right in *your* life? What does that mean to you? When is the right time for doing so?

> "It's suspiciously wonderful how a simple declaration of permission can be so freeing."
>
> — JILL BADONSKY,
> author and creativity coach

We often hear the phrase "take your time," but how often do we hear "take *your* time"? Allow this book to remind you: You can take time for yourself, making choices that serve *you* best. The ways in which you both use and perceive time are in your control. You also have choices about how you perceive the demands and pressures that make you *think* time is not your own. Time *is* yours, once you decide it is so.

It is helpful to remember the ways in which *others* benefit when you are taking control of your own time. The positive effects of taking your time have no other course but to ripple outward, affecting everybody in your circle: your family, your coworkers, your friends. Ironically, even though taking time for ourselves feels like taking time away from others, it actually is giving something back to them. Indeed, taking time for yourself allows you to *give back your best self.*

TIME AND PERMISSION

So, what gives us the right to "set our time right"? We give ourselves the right to do so! To make time our own, the first step is to give ourselves *permission* to liberate ourselves from the perceived pressures that control our time. When we do this, we open ourselves up to freedom. For many of us, the power of permission dates back to childhood, when we looked to parents and authority figures to "permit" us to do the things we wanted to do. A knee-jerk reaction to continue searching for permission stays with most of us into adulthood, especially when it comes to the things we do "just for us."

I remember reading the book *Living Juicy* years ago, in which author SARK suggested that we write ourselves a "permission slip" to be creative. Creating a physical representation of permission is indeed a powerful exercise. You might want to write a series of sentences or phrases that give you permission to take *your* time; you can refer to the sidebar "Permission Statements" for ideas.

You may even want to make a physical permission slip that illustrates your commitment to take *your* time, like the examples shown throughout this chapter.

Permission Statements

Here are some starter statements to explore in your journal:

- I deserve to take *my* time because _____.
- When I take *my* time, I am _____.
- I help others by taking *my* time because _____.
- I am allowed to take *my* time because _____.
- Taking control of *my* time is a good thing because _____.

As you start to take *your* time more often in life, it is common to come up against difficult feelings, such as guilt, lack, fear, questions of deservedness, and the like. If you have had a long-standing pattern of filling your time with obligations, responsibilities, "shoulds," and other things that drain your soul, it can be hard to break out of those ideas to realize that your time really *is* yours. Be gentle with yourself during this transition, and realize that you can take your time as you take *your* time.

Digital collage

Permission Slips by Karen Karsten

How does your permission slip feel to you? If, after creating your slip, you still are feeling resistance, guilt, or hesitation about taking *your* time, ask yourself: If someone *else* gave me this permission slip, would that change things? From whom, specifically, would this permission make a difference? These questions are helpful in identifying the sources that you feel — consciously or subconsciously — are withholding permission for you to live your fullest, best life.

"OURS" INSTEAD OF HOURS

As we've explored throughout this book, designing new ways to tell time helps us to *see* time in new ways. Creating a new clock that illustrates the ways in which you are taking *your* time is a very illuminating exercise. One suggestion I've used in workshops is to design a clock where you replace all the old "hours" with a different

Permission Slip by
Marney K. Makridakis

element. I suggest replacing the hours with "ours"; the "ours" represent all our cherished states of being, the beautiful things that are globally important to all of us. You'll see my list of suggested "ours" below.

After creating a new clock with new "ours," you can use it to tell time in a new, nonchronological way. For example, my "our" for 1:00 is "FUN." So, instead of seeing that now it's 1:00, we see that now it is FUN, which reminds us to measure the moment in *fun*, asking ourselves questions like these: What is fun about this moment? How might I make this moment *more* fun? Where is fun hiding in this moment?

If this approach intrigues you, here are my suggestions for new "ours" that serve as inspiring, enjoyable containers to hold and measure time:

1:00 — FUN!
- What is fun about this moment?
- How might I make this moment *more* fun?
- Where is fun hiding in this moment?

2:00 — YOU
- Who is sharing this moment with me?
- How authentically am I connecting with him/her/them?
- What might I have to offer and receive?

3:00 — CHI (the Chinese word for "energy")
- What does the energy around me feel like right now?
- What does the energy in my body feel like?
- How might I make better use of my energy right now?

4:00 — MORE
- How could I feel this moment more deeply?
- How could I appreciate this moment more?
- How could I be *more* aware?

5:00 — ALIVE

- What feels alive about this moment?
- What is alive and living around me?
- How might I inhabit this moment in a more alive way?

6:00 — KICKS

- How can I "get my kicks" and make this moment sillier?
- What can I laugh about?
- How might I help someone else laugh?

7:00 — HEAVEN

- What is divine about this moment?
- How does this moment point to the divine?
- How has divine timing led me to this moment?

8:00 — WAIT

- How would waiting and going slower change this moment?
- How might I incorporate stillness into this moment?
- What am I waiting for right now…how can I just go for it?

9:00 — MINE

- What would I like to keep from this moment?
- What memory would I like to savor forever?
- Right now, what is mine to do, and what is not?

10:00 — AGAIN

- What does this moment make me remember?
- What is important about this memory?
- What would I want to remember about this moment, later?

Digital collage

Our New Ours
by Marney K. Makridakis

11:00 — REVVIN'
- How is this moment revving up my engine?
- Where do I need to take action?
- How efficiently is my personal engine running, right now?

12:00 — DELVE
- How can I dig deeper into this moment?
- What is hidden beneath the surface?
- How fully am I encompassing all the layers of this moment?

If these new time delineators resonate with you, I encourage you to give them a try in your everyday life. Even in the most unpleasant circumstances, you can challenge yourself to tap into feeling more positive emotions. Tara Douglas-Smith said,

I have loved adopting these new "ours" into my life. I integrated the words into a regular clock, so that I could see them when I'm checking "normal" time. I love checking the clock now, because I'm always surprised as the "our" always gives a little gift! It is helping me to always find something wonderful to take away in any moment. I could be doing something unpleasant at noon, but then I realize it's Delve O'Clock, so then I know I have to dig deeper to find more meaning in the moment. The amazing thing is that it *always* works. The only time it doesn't work is when I forget to check the "our." With this exercise, life has become effervescently alive. This is my favorite way to tell time!

With this method, you'll find that you can't wait to "watch the clock," because you never know what surprise you might find when you look to see what time it *really* is. After a while, you won't even need your clock to remind you, because you'll automatically have these new hourly associations ingrained in you!

ARTsignment: Clock of Ours

Whether you use the above suggestions for new "ours" or design your own interpretation, creating a new clock is an empowering way to design time. For this ARTsignment, you'll give yourself permission to design a new clock based on a new kind of time…*your* time.

Step 1: Design a new clock for yourself that demonstrates a new way to tell time. Feel free to use my "ours" as the basis of your clock, or you can create your own "ours," or even use an entirely different approach for your time-tracking method. The gallery that follows includes examples of all these approaches that you can refer to for inspiration.

Step 2: As you work on your clock, really *see yourself* living a new life, in which you are guided by your new choices in time. How will your new clock change things? What will your new life look like?

Step 3: Place your clock where you can see it often, giving yourself permission to "tell time" in new ways. If you like this method, you may want to create multiple copies of your clock and put them in several strategic locations. You may even find that you want to create clocks for specific purposes, such as a marriage clock, a parenting clock, a work clock, or a downtime clock.

ARTsignment Gallery: Clock of Ours

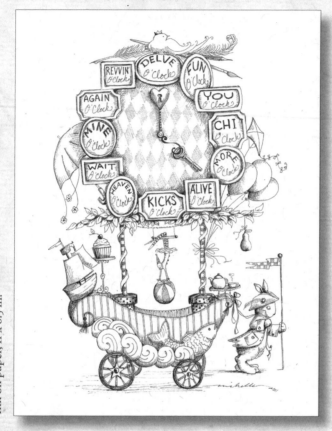

Ink on paper, 11 x 8.5 in.

"After introducing the idea of 'ours' into my head and illustrating it in a whimsical sketch, I found I began to mark time a bit differently. I created my own version of this clock, which gives me a prompt to recall the new words for each hour, and it makes me smile! This ARTsignment has moved me to assign a fun little ritual to each hour. I believe that marking time in this new way will give me a sense of a fully celebrated day!"

— MICHELLE BERLIN

ARTsignment Gallery: Clock of Ours

Digital collage

"I created this clock for Marney's workshop over three years ago, and looking at it now, it still gives me a feeling of relief. My clock reflects living in the moment, the present, instead of being hindered by the confines of a twelve-hour clock. Time here is measured nonlinearly in love, growth, art, sleep, and rebirth. In this clock, time is represented as never ending, so there is no need to worry about the future, because the future will always be there. Our place in the universe is guaranteed and limitless when we don't sit and worry about past and future. We certainly have to make plans for the future, but we need to live in the now, in the moment. Accepting where we are and using this moment to work on our dreams makes time feel like it is expanding and will never end."   — WILLIAM J. CHARLEBOIS

ARTsignment Gallery: Clock of Ours

Digital collage

"The circular image was taken from a photo of a movie reel, because time always tells a story. Since time can function as a way to return to events or move forward to new experiences, I chose a variety of different types of doors to represent the "ours." I used Marney's 'our' prompts to incorporate meaningful imagery into the clock: 3:00 (chi) is an image of my daughter dancing, 8:00 (create) is a potter's wheel, 11:00 (revvin) is my husband's guitar. I am a happier person now that I am open to a variety of ways to perceive and experience time. With this clock, I can now ask myself, 'Can I view this experience, this interaction, this space of time in any other way?' The answer is almost always YES!"

— SHARON B. GORBERG

ARTsignment Gallery: Clock of Ours

Acrylic on LP record, 12 x 12 in.

"This clock was made out of an old 33-1/3 record. It has been painted in a mandala-style design, which is soothing to me. Every hour has a word that I can focus on for a positive affirmation each hour. This clock helps me see the importance of letting go of saying, '*If* I could view time this way…' and start to say, 'I *will* look at time this way! I believe I will start today…I will take MY time!'" — PATRICIA J. MOSCA

SECTION 3

INTEGRATION AND INSPIRATION

15. TIME DESIGN IN EVERYDAY LIFE

Poetic Pause

Time as baby's hands
Grasping at all within reach
To make sense of Now

Grab your schedules and calendars, because now we'll take everything you've explored in this book and apply it directly to your life. We're going to look at your individual life circumstances and transform them with your favorite time creation techniques. You'll learn several simple tools to help facilitate this process, including these:

- Weekly Time Check
- Time Transcendence "Ticks and Talks"
- Portraitizing Instead of Prioritizing
- Time Design Diagnosis Chart
- STARTsignment Questions

WEEKLY TIME CHECK

As discussed in chapter 13, *anticipation* plays a key role in transforming time. For example, when we become more aware of the tasks or activities that dissipate our energy, we can anticipate them and control our perception of time, especially during those moments. We can also anticipate the meaningful moments — the "good times" and the "important times" — so that we're consciously aware of those moments when they happen and less likely to say, "Whoa, where did the time go?" after they are gone.

A Weekly Time Check simply consists of looking at your calendar for the upcoming week and pinpointing the moments, events, and occasions that might benefit from a bit of *conscious time creation*. It's as simple as glancing through your schedule to anticipate the times when it could be helpful to apply the tools you've learned in this book.

As you look through your calendar or appointment book, here are some things you might want to note:

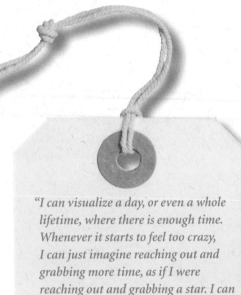

"I can visualize a day, or even a whole lifetime, where there is enough time. Whenever it starts to feel too crazy, I can just imagine reaching out and grabbing more time, as if I were reaching out and grabbing a star. I can remember that there really, really is enough. Always. And it's right here at my fingertips."

— TERRI ST. CLOUD, artist

- Events you're looking forward to
- Events you're dreading
- Things you're nervous or unsure about
- Deadlines or due dates
- Moments when you think you'd like time to move faster
- Moments when you think you'd like time to move slower
- Places in your schedule where you wish you had more time
- Activities that are engaging
- Activities that are boring

You may even want to develop a key word or a simple doodle or symbol for each, and add those symbols or words into your datebook or calendar as a reminder to apply the time creation techniques from this book to help you achieve desired results in these crucial moments. To connect to your intuitive wisdom on this subject, simply ask your Time Guide, "Which concepts would be most helpful to me in this situation?" Your Time Guide, speaking through your intuition, will always guide you appropriately. For further inspiration, you can also refer to the Time Design Diagnosis Chart, later in this chapter.

TIME TRANSCENDENCE "TICKS AND TALKS"

When you do your Weekly Time Check, pay attention to moments when you anticipate wanting to control the flow of time, making your perception of its movement either faster or slower. When you see one of these moments in your calendar or datebook, put a tick mark next to it to remind you to call upon the Time Transcendence Tools from chapter 3, which are summarized here in the sidebar "Time Transcendence Tools." If you have some colored markers available, an easy technique is to use a green mark to indicate events and circumstances when you would like time to move faster, and a red mark to indicate when you would like time to move more slowly.

You can also integrate the Time Transcendence Tools into your daily life by talking about them with the people with whom you'll be spending time. For example, you might discuss some of the Time Transcendence Tools for speeding up time with a coworker before you embark on a mundane task together. Or you might discuss the tools for slowing down time with your

Time Transcendence Tools

Here is a review of the Time Transcendence Tools presented in chapter 3:

Time Transcendence Tools: Slowing Time

- Create focused time rather than scattered time.
- Focus on segmentation rather than wholeness.
- Create a Time Wrap.
- Slow down.
- Place yourself in circular time.
- Connect with your senses.
- Notice *everything* happening.
- Take mental snapshots.
- Engage in activities of high time awareness.
- Tithe your time.

Time Transcendence Tools: Speeding Up Time

- Create scattered time rather than focused time.
- Focus on wholeness rather than segmentation.
- Connect to your passion.
- Look for lessons.
- Engage in physical movement.
- Engage in mental movement.
- Fill yourself up.
- Pass the remote.
- Connect with others.
- Time-lapse yourself.

family prior to a vacation, to ensure that you all make the most out of your time together.

PORTRAITIZING INSTEAD OF PRIORITIZING

The third tool invites you to *portraitize* rather than prioritize. Prioritizing involves looking at "what is most important," but as discussed earlier in the book, often the very act of evaluating what is most important can just lead to *more* overwhelm. Prioritizing is a linear process, an either/or process. It means choosing, and for better or worse, it's in our human nature to resist choosing. Portraitizing, on the other hand, allows us to create each day as a work of art, capitalizing on what we most love about ourselves and the world around us, allowing these forces to guide our time choices. Portraitizing combines several of the concepts in this book into one single planning method that integrates directly and practically into our day-to-day lives. Rather than being linear and static like a list of priorities, portraitizing is fluid, changing, and malleable. Like a work of art, portraitizing evolves and changes along with our inspiration.

The utility of the portraitizing process is very flexible. You can create one "portrait" for your general life or use it as a regular time creation tool, whereby each morning you spend a few moments portraitizing your day. One technique that works well is to purchase a bound tablet of index cards and create a portrait on a new card every day. It doesn't take much time, and it is a wonderful way to ground yourself each morning and bridge your time creation techniques with your daily reality.

Here are instructions for the portraitizing process. You can refer to the diagram on the next page as you create your portrait:

1. Turn your writing surface in a horizontal position.
2. First, create the *landscape*. In the upper third of your page, start writing all the things that you want and need to do, as you think of them. If you like, break outside of writing in straight lines and columns; write in curved lines, let each item go in a different direction, and add little doodles and decorations. Let your mind wander and flow as you allow

all those ideas, thoughts, responsibilities, and inklings to be put down on paper.

This "landscape" of your portrait is the *broad view* of all the thoughts and ideas dancing around in your mind. This exercise in and of itself is helpful; I find it's a very freeing way to address the knotted-up ideas in my head, allowing them to unravel on paper. Like a physical landscape, the landscape area in your portrait can evolve and change; you can continue to add to your landscape of ideas and endeavors throughout the day, as you are inspired to do so.

3. Create your *focal point*. Prioritizing focuses on what you have to do, but portraitizing places greater emphasis on who you want to *be*. In the center of your page, write one to three words that describe how you most want to *feel* today, and place them in a circle. These words could be the same each day you do this process, or they might change from day to day, based on your mood, desire, and daily needs. This circle is your *focal point*. Having a focal point helps you know what to focus on. It's the same as with a work of art: the canvas can contain a very rich landscape, with intricacies and complexity, but the focal point is what holds your vision.

LANDSCAPE

(the evolving collection of "things to do")

FOCAL POINT

(one to three words to describe
how you most want to feel)

STILL LIFE   LIGHT SOURCE

(daily plan to be still   (core motivators and ideas
and refuel yourself)   to activate them)

Portraitizing Diagram

Your focal point serves as a visual reminder of what is most important, even as you continue to build your landscape with other thoughts and ideas that come to mind. Refer to your focal point throughout the day, as you move through your "landscape." With your focus defined on *being* rather than doing, it becomes easier to tune in to your intuition and see the doors that may be opening for you. When your day is ruled by a list of things to do, it's more challenging to connect viscerally to the mysterious gifts of time, such as inner relativity, synchronicity, and divine timing.

4. Add the *light source*. Your light source is the energy that motivates you. It is your gesture of passion, your channel of purpose. In the lower-right corner, write or draw words or symbols that represent your light source. You might also jot down some ideas for how to activate that light source. You might write down ideas for bringing more joy to your workday — for example: blow bubbles, play music, take dance breaks, work outside. Even when your landscape contains things that you may not necessarily love doing, you can still flood your day with light and radiance. Remember: time is always "told" through our perspective of any given experience.

5. Add the *still life*. In the lower-left corner, write a few words or make a small drawing or doodle that serves as a reminder for your still-life time: what you will do every day to nurture your spirit. Sometimes getting things done means doing less. When we take the time to feed our spirit with love, we can truly use the endless power of that very love to help transform time and live our fullest lives. No matter how busy we are, we can take time to *be still* in small, easy, doable ways that transform how we move through time and time moves through us.

On the next page is an example of a portrait that I completed for one of my days.

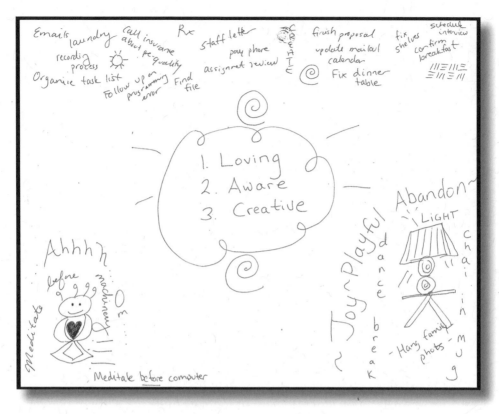

Portraitizing Example

TIME DESIGN DIAGNOSIS CHART

All the concepts in this book are very flexible and can be used in a variety of ways to help you create a new sense of time. As stated earlier in this chapter, your intuition is your best tool for guidance, especially when you access that intuition through the voice of your Time Guide.

If you'd like some additional guidance, the following Time Design Diagnosis Chart offers ideas for which ARTsignments I've found to be most relevant to a variety of popular time concerns and challenges. Here are some statements about time, as made directly by my workshop participants. Each of these common complaints and challenges corresponds to a number, which you can refer to in the Time Design Diagnosis Chart for specific ARTsignment recommendations:

1. "I feel as if time is just slipping away from me. I don't feel like I have anything to show for my time."
2. "I have to spend a lot of time doing things that I don't want to do."
3. "I'd pursue my dream if I had more time."
4. "I don't have time to take care of myself."
5. "My days just feel like I'm constantly running around: everything is just rush, rush, rush."
6. "I'm always worried about the past or the future, and find it hard to live in the moment."
7. "Worries, regret, and pain from my past affect my experience of the present."
8. "I don't have a realistic sense of time. I'm always procrastinating and am never sure how long things take."
9. "I'm afraid I'm just going through the motions and not really living."
10. "I'm consumed with deadlines and external pressures, which make it impossible to do the things I really want to do."
11. "It seems like time moves too fast or too slow, and I feel a loss of power."
12. "I really like the idea of transforming time, but I just can't see how it could actually work in my life, which seems to be monopolized by linear time."

After selecting the statements most relevant to you, you can refer directly to the ARTsignments indicated in the chart. The two introductory ARTsignments (ARTernity Box and Time Guide) are especially malleable and are effective in addressing *all* the concerns listed here.

COMPLAINT	ARTernity Box	Time Guide	Wellativity Art	Create Your Kairos	Flow Chart	GratiTimeline	A Chime for Love	A New Rituality	Stop. Watch.	Metaphor-morphosis	One Day Life/Time	Synchronicity Watch	Calendure	Clock of Ours
1	X	X				X						X		
2	X	X			X		X							
3	X	X					X			X				
4	X	X						X						X
5	X	X						X	X					
6	X	X			X								X	
7	X	X								X	X			
8	X	X									X		X	
9	X	X				X						X		
10	X	X							X					X
11	X	X	X	X										
12	X	X	X	X										

Time Design Diagnosis Chart

STARTsignment Questions

After you complete each of the ARTsignments in this book, they will continue to en-rich you as you reflect on them and integrate the concepts into your daily life. Here is a list of STARTsignment questions, which are starter prompts to initiate further reflection and integration of your ARTsignment experiences as you create time in your daily life. You can explore any question at any given moment to deeply anchor your experience with the ARTsignments that you have completed.

ARTernity Box

- How are my current ideas about time influencing this moment?
- Are my current ideas about time limiting me in any way?
- What new choices and beliefs could I make about time that might help me right now?

Time Guide

- How might my Time Guide support me today?
- What do my Time Guide and I have to celebrate today?
- What does my Time Guide want me to know about this moment?

Wellativity Art

- How is the equation "Fulfillment = Time + Imagination^2" relevant to me right now?
- How can my imagination help me in this moment?
- Which Time Transcendence Tools could I employ to make time seem to be moving slower or faster at my will?

Create Your Kairos

- Am I in *kronos* or *kairos* right now, or a combination?
- Would I like to make a different choice?
- How might this event be seen differently through kairos eyes?

Flow Chart

- How might I bring more "flow essences" into this moment?
- How might this moment benefit from circular time?
- How might I create more time for flow in my life?

GratiTimeline

- How might I include more gratitude into my perception of this moment?
- How might I become more aware of and thankful for the passing hours?

- What is *appreciating* through time in this moment? What aspect of myself or my life is gaining in value today?

A Chime for Love

- How might I bring more focus onto what I love in this moment?
- How might I live two times at once in this moment, just by changing my focus?
- How might I bring the dependability of love into this moment?

A New Rituality

- How did I welcome the day today? How did it feel?
- How might I bring peaceful closure to this day?
- How could ritual expand my sense of this moment?

Stop. Watch.

- When did I "stop and watch" today?
- Do I have unplanned moments in my schedule? How might I bring more in?
- What can I do to ensure that I have still, unplanned moments each day?

Metaphor-morphosis

- In what ways is my metaphor helping me today?
- In what ways could I call upon my metaphor to help me more, or differently?
- What other metaphor could I call in to assist me right now?

One Day Life/Time

- If my whole life consisted of just one day, how would that change my experience of this moment?
- Is there anything that I'm putting off for "one day"?
- What might motivate me to make "one day" be *today*?

Synchronicity Watch

- What connections am I noticing from my Synchronicity Watch?
- How is my awareness of synchronicity strengthening my intuition?
- Are there any hunches or connections I'd like to follow up on?

Calendure

- How has energetic planning helped me today?
- How might energetic planning help me tomorrow?
- What events would be aided by energetic planning?

Clock of Ours

- What role does permission play in taking back my time?
- If I take time for myself, how does that help others?
- What time is it right now, according to my Clock of Ours? What new layer of meaning does the current "our" bring to this moment?

16. CREATE YOUR OWN ARTsignments

Poetic Pause

Time as a paintbrush
Colors the canvas of life
Spilling surprises

Throughout this book, you have been engaging in ARTsignments to transport you in a time machine of sorts, allowing you to travel deeply into the full dimensions of time and extend the breadth of its meaning and experience. You can take the power of ARTsignments even further by designing your own!

Here are some simple tips and suggestions, if you are interested in creating your own ARTsignments:

1. Start with a summary: simply summarize your time-related challenges in a few sentences.
2. Try taking your own words literally. In ARTbundance coaching, trainees learn how to take their clients' words *literally* to create ARTsignments. For example, if a client talks about wanting to "get out of the box," the coach can create an ARTsignment that embodies that idea (such as a three-dimensional self-portrait outside of a box). If the client keeps talking about being "stuck," the coach might look at how this could be interpreted as a literal project (for example, invite her to create

a "stuck"-themed collage using alternatives to glue, like bubble gum, toothpaste, or jam). The same process is true as you give yourself your own ARTsignment about time. Look at your own words *literally*, and see what ideas come to mind.

3. Apply creativity. Think of a way that you might apply creativity to the challenge and create a solution or explore a new outlook or approach.

To help get you started, refer to the sidebars in this section, which suggest ways to apply the elements of art and writing to your time challenges.

4. Give yourself permission to think of "bad" ideas. Not every idea you have for an ARTsignment will be a "good" one. Some of your ideas will be boring, awkward, nonsensical, and rather goofy (such as my very silly idea above, about using jam as an adhesive in a collage!). The more ideas you allow yourself to have, the more ideas you will have. And the more ideas you have, the more often you'll come across an idea that really does work! Be patient, *time your time*, and enjoy the process.

5. Track your ideas. Develop a method for keeping track of your ARTsignment ideas, such as a notebook, note card file, or handheld tape recorder. Make the effort to write them all down, so that you can always

---

Create Your Own ARTsignment: Applying Art to Challenges

Here are some suggestions for ways to add the element of art to the time challenge you are working on:

- Make a collage
- Create a painting
- Work with clay or dough
- Take photographs
- Work with fabric or needlework
- Draw with any variety of supplies (pencils, markers, crayons, lipstick, and so on)
- Draw with your nondominant hand or do "blind contour drawing," where you don't look at what you are drawing
- Try digital art
- Make a paper doll
- Create a temporary sculpture with household items (soup cans, desk supplies, and so on)
- Draw with chalk on the sidewalk
- Create a self-portrait with any media
- Create portraits of other people with any media
- Reinvent or alter any of the ARTsignments you created from this book

come back to your ideas later for further reference or expansion.

I'm delighted to present inspiring examples created by four women who took these suggestions to heart and designed their own original ARTsignments to transform their biggest time challenges. In the sections that follow, you'll see the ARTsignments they created, paired with an intimate look into their thought process. Each artist also presents step-by-step directions for her ARTsignment so that you can give it a try. I hope that these original projects inspire you to design your own ARTsignments as well!

"Imagination is like a trampoline that you can use to jump above your situation so that you can grasp something new and wonderful that you can't quite reach from where you are standing in the midst of your challenge."

— RAE SHAGALOV,
ARTbundance Coach

ORIGINAL ARTSIGNMENT:
BUILD YOUR OWN TIME-TRAVELING DEVICE
by Marguerite Bryant

One of my biggest challenges with time is a fear of getting older and not being able to accomplish all that I want to do in my lifetime. I'm forty-six and seem to be going through a bit of a midlife crisis. I'm finding that I have a lot less energy these days, so I am looking for ways to make the most of what I have, as well as ways to create more energy, all while keeping my dreams alive and afloat.

Thinking in fanciful and childlike ways has really helped to keep my spirits up during all of the changes I am going through. That was how I came up with the idea for my Time-Traveling Tub. I currently do not have a bathtub, and for years I have been longing for an antique claw-foot tub. One of my favorite pastimes is taking long bubble baths. The warm water puts me into such a wonderful state of relaxation, and I have the most delicious daydreams, where anything is possible. I lose myself for a little while, and all my problems dissolve. Deep relaxation is the perfect atmosphere for planting and growing dreams!

Here is the illustration I made for my Time-Traveling Tub and the poem I wrote about it:

Watercolor and pen on paper, 8 x 9 in.

Time-Traveling Tub by Marguerite Bryant

Time-Traveling Tub

She journeys the world
In a time-traveling tub
It goes really fast
So planes she does snub
She's been many places
And she's met lots of folks
Between destinations
Computer keys she pokes
Writing books of her adventures
Is what she loves to do

So look way up
Into the sky
And she may be flying
Over you!
She'll blow you a rainbow
Soap bubble kiss
And if it lands upon your nose
You'll receive your dearest wish!
Everybody loves her
And well she knows it
When she reaches her destination
LOVE
She shows it
To every creature
That crosses her path
She exhales peace
And she inhales wrath
You just never know
Where next she will go
But joy she will bring
'Cause she loves everything!

How to Create Your Own Time-Traveling Device

1. Complete these journal questions:

- When do you feel most relaxed? (If possible, do the thing that makes you lose yourself to relaxation, and then answer the rest of these questions from that ultimate state of relaxation.)
- What do you always say you want to do but never seem to get around to?

Create Your Own ARTsignment: Applying Creative Writing to Challenges

Here are some suggestions for ways to add the element of creative writing to the time challenge you are working on:

- Answer journal prompts
- Write a haiku
- Write a short story
- Write a memoir or personal essay
- Write a rhyming poem
- Write an abstract poem
- Write a miniscreenplay
- Write song lyrics
- Rewrite lyrics to a song
- Write a poem with "found" words (random words from a book page, for example)
- Write a letter to someone/something
- Write a letter *from* someone/something (in that person's voice)
- Write in a made-up language
- Write with your nondominant hand
- Write with unconventional writing supplies

- What are the obstacles that keep you from doing these things you've always wanted to do? What if you had a magical device that made all of your obstacles disappear?

2. Go to a childlike place in your mind where anything is possible, just for fun! It might help to imagine yourself as a child. Remember when you were a kid and things didn't have to be realistic or logical? Close your eyes and daydream, *and let your time-traveling device come to you.* Be patient while the artist child inside of you assembles your unique vehicle.

3. When you see your time-traveling device clearly, use your art supplies of choice to illustrate it. If you like, you can write a story or poem about it.

4. Place your time-traveling device where you will see it often, and allow yourself to ponder it daily. Inspired ideas will slowly grow and blossom during your pondering periods.

Here are some things you might ponder:

- Imagine you can get into your time-traveling device and go somewhere. Where do you go and what is it like? (The more you go there in your mind, the more likely you will go there in reality!)
- How does your time-traveling device address the obstacles that keep you from living your dreams?
- How might you use what you've discovered in the creation and pondering of this time-traveling device to overcome the obstacles to your dreams?

Enjoy your journeys in your time-traveling device. I'll wave to you from my tub!

ORIGINAL ARTsignment:
A REAL TIME SAVOR: A LIFE-ALTARING STUDY
by TiCo

My biggest challenge with time is incorporating what I call Sacred Mindless Time into each day, without guilt. I require a lot of empty time to hear that tiny whisper inside that sends me creative ideas. One of my favorite things to do in life is to channel ideas and figure out how to manifest them, since they don't yet have a set of instructions. It takes a lot of trial and error, failure and success, constructing, deconstructing, and reconstructing until the creation is finally complete. And this process takes time and patience. After reading about Marney's creative concepts of time, I can now identify that my process takes *kairos* time! I can't *kronos* when I'm creating! Relaxation and empty mind are requirements for my idea-manifestation process. I find the creative process to be a form of meditation and even a form of prayer, and being stuck to a clock makes for rather stressful meditation or prayer!

After devouring the Create Your Kairos ARTsignment, I took some kairos time and did some journaling. I made three different entries on three separate pages: one for my past experience/training of time, one about any future shifts about time, and one about what I can do in the present to incorporate more sacred kairos idea-manifesting time into each day.

From journaling, an idea came to create my own ARTsignment to help me incorporate all-important sacred kairos time into my day. It's called A Real Time Savor: A Life Altaring Study. The object of this ARTsignment is to treat my time like a gourmet meal — to slow down and savor every bite of it instead of rushing through my day, not fully tasting every moment. I decided to do this by making a shrine and creating a sacred altar space to honor kairos/kronos awareness.

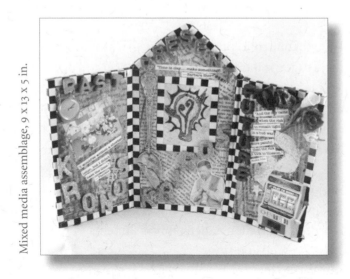

Mixed media assemblage, 9 x 13 x 5 in.

A Real Time Savor Shrine by TiCo

My altar space is next to my bed, so that I can start the day at the altar focusing with intent to add kairos time to it. At the end of my day, I can reflect on how the intended kairos time affected or improved my day. Or if it didn't happen, I can explore what I can do differently to keep it consistent. The sacred altar space is a personal, peaceful sanctuary to go to whenever comfort and reflection are needed. The altar activity choices are many: journaling, meditating, prayer, reflection, dialoguing, and so on.

I tried this process for a few weeks, and I found that starting each day in my altar space and making the intention to add kairos time to each day has manifested more original creations than I have ever been able to complete before! A home filled with UFOs (unfinished objects) is now becoming more of a gallery of finished pieces. I have had guilt over mindless time for decades. To some, it may appear as if we're not doing anything at all when we're in kairos time, but kairos exploration, intention, and reflection have made a major breakthrough in a very stuck area of my life…and it's been only a few weeks!

How to Create Your Own Real Time Savor

If you find yourself similarly stuck and craving Sacred Mindless Time, you can make your own version of A Real Time Savor: A Life-Altaring Study. Here are some general steps to help you give it a try:

1. Journal about your concept of time, now that you've read this book. Try writing one page for the past, one for the future, and one for the present.
2. Cut three pieces of stiff material for the base of your shrine. These will represent past, present, and future. I used foam core, but you can use any medium that speaks to your heart (such as wood, metal, or stiff fabric interfacing). Put the base pieces together to be the base of your shrine.
3. Tear your journal entries into strips and attach them to the base of the shrine in any way you please, and embellish as you like. I added paints and gel medium, and then added embellishments to represent my feelings of past, present, and future.
4. Place your shrine in a special area where you can go for peace and reflection. Add items around your shrine to build an altar setting. Keep

a journal and pen nearby for easy reflection in your altar area. Make a commitment to spend time in this space regularly.

I hope you find A Real Time Savor to be "life altaring" and that it allows you to savor each moment of every day with intention and presence.

ORIGINAL ARTsignment: MISSION TREE OVERLAY
by Violette Clark

My biggest challenge with time is that I keep thinking there's not enough time and feeling like I need to clone myself. I've realized that it really is a case of saying yes to too many things that are not that important. I have a fear of disappointing too many people, so I continually say yes rather than weighing whether or not the request is in keeping with my values and goals. When I was reading *First Things First*, by Stephen R. Covey et al., I was moved by the graphical image of a tree with mission, roles, and principles placed on it. The idea of rooting myself in these ideals really resonated with me, so I created my own version of a mission tree to help me address my time in an inspiring way.

Mixed media on paper, 10.5 x 8.25 in.

The Mission Tree Overlay is a tool to help me take back control of my time and realize that I can use my time doing what is most important to me. My mission is to inspire women and teens to embrace who they are through the vehicle of their creativity. I have learned to use my Mission Tree Overlay *before* I say yes to anything. I ask myself, does the request fit into my values, goals, and dreams? If not, then I simply will say no. I have to say no to certain

Mission Tree Overlay by Violette Clark

things in order to be free and available for projects that feed my soul and the souls of the people I'm here to serve. If my Mission Tree can't overlay the request and be a good fit, then I need to be saying "No thanks."

How to Create Your Own Mission Tree Overlay

1. Do some free thinking and journaling about what truly matters to you and how you most want to use your time.
2. Draw a sketch of a tree on a blank sheet of paper.
3. In the branches, write down a list of the roles that you play and that you want to play in your life.
4. On the trunk of the tree, write down your mission: a statement that summarizes your purpose.
5. In the roots, write your principles and values.
6. Continue to decorate and embellish your tree in any way you like.
7. You now have a tool to use whenever requests, invitations, or opportunities come your way. Lay your mission tree over the request, and see if it matches up. This offers clarity for your answer, so that you can say yes or no with confidence.

ORIGINAL ARTSIGNMENT: THE ARCHITECT OF TIME
by Sandi Wedemeier

One of my biggest desires is to have a smooth, flowing experience of time. I tended to fill my calendar and take on more projects and commitments than I really had time for. I also tended to underestimate the amount of time needed to complete things that were on my calendar, and I didn't delegate time to leisure activities.

To help me with this challenge, I created an ARTsignment called the Architect of Time. This phrase had been resonating and rattling around in both my unconscious and conscious mind for better than two years, but I never really knew what it meant. Through this ARTsignment, the meaning is finally clear: *I* am the architect of time, and *I* am the one who creates the blueprint for my time. This is a new lens, a new frame for understanding. For the longest time, I've been experiencing time as something sharp and pointy, all angles and static. I was overbooked and overcommitted, with no time for even a meal that wasn't eaten in front of the computer. Leisure time? Time for fun and to spend with friends? Maybe an hour or two here and there, but time just for me was at a premium. I felt I had to say yes to anyone or anything asking for my time.

I came to a point where some of my commitments were coming to an end, and I started taking a really honest look at all the places to which I had committed myself. I realized that some of these things really didn't serve me. I let go of both the internal and external pressures exerted on *my time* and made my time my priority. Right now, I'm still detoxing from chronic busyness. It is the right thing to now experience time as expansive and flowing, with hours that are there just to be. I am learning what it means to *blueprint my time*, what it means to consider myself in my schedule. I'm still in the expansiveness of it all but am moving toward a new understanding of time and a new way of being with time. A visual image of the Architect of Time is guiding me in this journey.

Mixed media on paper, 12 x 8 in.

The Architect of Time by Sandi Wedemeier

How to Create Your Own Architect of Time

1. Answer these questions, following your intuition; just go with the first answers that bubble up.

   - How do I experience time now?
   - What would I prefer time to feel like?
   - What sensations would I give the passage of time?
   - What symbols represent time to me?
   - If I were the Architect of Time, how might I experience time differently?

2. The next step is to create your own Architect of Time. Start collecting images that represent time to you in a concrete way, both literally and metaphorically. Find either a photograph of yourself or an image of a person with whom you closely identify. Look for images, single words, and phrases that bring about the new sensations you wish to have about time. Now, just start playing! Place the image that represents you in the center of your page, and start filling in the spaces around it with the images that lend themselves to this new experience of time for you. Keep moving images around, adding and subtracting until your intuition tells you it's just right.

3. Keep this collage in your office; or scan, reduce, and print the image to tuck into your appointment book to remind yourself that *you* are the Architect of Time and you can blueprint time in any way you like.

PREFACE

(or, The End Is Really the Beginning)

When you create time in your own image, time becomes a whimsical spiral; the preface can come at the end, because truly, any end is just the beginning. Everything you've created through this book is malleable and changeable, like time itself. All your ARTsignments are works in progress. Please alter and adapt each one as you need to. You may even want to create a final piece of artwork to visually summarize your insights and experiences.

I invite you to return to your ARTernity Box from chapter 1 and review the slips of paper containing your initial impressions about time. Here are the questions presented in the first chapter:

1. When you think about time, what is the first thing that comes to mind?
2. What is your deepest wish, regarding time?
3. What is your biggest challenge, regarding time?
4. Do you spend more time wishing time would speed up or go more slowly? Why?
5. If you had more time, how might your life be different?

6. If you knew you had less time on this earth, how might your life be different?

7. If you suddenly never had to worry about time, how might your life be different?

8. What methods have you used to keep track of your time (calendars, smartphones, online calendars, datebooks, and so on)? Which methods work best for you? Which seem to be least effective?

9. Do you wear a watch? Why or why not?

10. What was "time" like in your house when you were growing up? What beliefs did your parents and/or other family members have about time, and how were those beliefs manifested in their actions?

11. How is your current experience of time related to these patterns and observations from your childhood?

12. What drew you to this book?

After reviewing your answers, pose one more question to yourself: What has changed since you began this book? Make note of any significant shifts, changes, new thoughts, and new perceptions, as well as any new questions about time. What comes next in *your* time design?

Mixed media, 6.5 x 6.5 x 3.5 in.

ARTernity Box ARTsignment by Jennifer Walling

Jennifer Walling's ARTernity Box, a hatbox that she transformed into a working clock, is shown here. She shares the timeless nature of this journey: "I continue to add more insights to my box. It is an ongoing process that continues to teach me. Everything in its own time."

The world of creativity is an eternity in and of itself. Through your imagination, *you are always, and infinitely, timeless.*

ACKNOWLEDGMENTS

*I*f I made a GratiTimeline to represent every individual who has helped make this book a reality, it would be a very long and colorful chain!

Georgia Hughes, my editor, blessed me with enthusiasm, expertise, and gentle guidance in publishing this book, and I am thankful to the entire team at New World Library for an extraordinarily delightful publishing experience. Special thanks to Elissa Rabellino for her helpful copyediting and deft ability to get inside my head and understand what I want to say; Kristen Cashman for her amazing attention to detail and heartfelt commitment to every single step of the project; Kim Corbin for the helpful marketing efforts and guidance; and especially Tracy Cunningham, Tona Pearce Myers, and the rest of the design team for giving such special attention to the unconventional design and layout of the book.

This book includes the contributions of eighty amazing individuals whose art and stories grace these pages; this really is their book, too. I am deeply honored by their creations and the extraordinary optimism and flexibility each person offered as we pulled this book together. Special thanks to Patricia Mosca, Michelle Berlin, and Marilyn Harris Mills, who went above and beyond, and kept asking for (and giving me) more and more ARTsignments and stories. I am deeply inspired by the original ARTsignments created by Marguerite Bryant, Violette Clark, TiCo, and Sandi Wedemeier. Big thanks also go to Sharon Gorberg, whose beautiful clock design inspired the cover art.

I offer huge thanks and sing-outs to anyone who has ever worked on the Artella Team — past, present, and future — for all they have done to make Artella Land come alive and make my daily life so much more joyful, fun, and meaningful. I am especially thankful to Paula Swenson and Cheryl Richards for brilliant assistance in coordinating and managing so many behind-the-scenes details for the production of this book, in addition to their other roles in Artella Land. Special thanks to Annette Phillips, who designed many of the decorative elements on these pages, and to Tammy Hensley, who helped me design the Metaphor Machine worksheets and created all the da Vinci–themed clocks seen throughout the book.

I am so appreciative of Ken Evoy and the team at SiteSell.com, for products and services that are both time-savers and sanity savers. I am thankful to Kevin Roberts and "Lovemarks," which has deeply influenced the way I approach all aspects of my work.

I am grateful to all participants in the "From Here to ARTernity" workshops, whose affirmative feedback showed me that these crazy techniques actually work, with a special nod to Bill Charlebois for all the positive, helpful vibes.

The trainees, coaches, and practitioners in the ARTbundance community have made contributions not only to this book but also to the ARTbundance philosophy and the ARTsignments practice at large. This community is my daily creative oxygen.

My parents brought writing, art, and creative thinking into my entire life and being, beginning in young childhood and continuing through today. My mother, Arthiss Kliever, offered constant cheerleading during this book's creation and utilized her librarian skills to assist me in a variety of research tasks for this book. And even though my father, Lonnie Kliever, is no longer on this earth, I thank him for continuing to show up when I need him, especially when I am writing.

My sister, Launa Kliever, has offered a lifetime of love and friendship, and I am especially thankful for two lessons from her that were in my mind almost constantly while writing this book: "the zoomie car game" and "never throw a watercolor away."

My darling and daring little son, Kai, is the sublime personification of kairos time, and I am blessed by his stories and inspirations that fill many pages of this book and every inch of my heart.

I enjoy the presence of so many talented Muses in my life who continually inspire and champion my creativity, especially Brian Andreas, Kathy Cano-Murillo, Laurie Gough, and Tama Kieves. Marci Shimoff, a longtime personal hero, gifted this book with her inspiring foreword and continues to motivate me with her groundbreaking, visionary work in the realms of personal happiness and unconditional love, as well as the authentic ways in which she integrates those concepts into her life. The fabulous Susan Ariel Rainbow Kennedy connected me to New World Library, as well as to so many other joy-filled personal and professional adventures, and my heart is filled with joyful appreciation for it all. Jill Badonsky's advice, humor, and celebration helped me immensely throughout the writing of this book. I loved being "book pregnant" at the same time!

The WOW group has offered years of support that echoed so loudly in my heart as I was writing this book: Diane Armstrong, Ann Fisher, Melissa Daimler, and Terry Jordan. I am also appreciative of Jennifer Louden for making the group happen.

I am humbled by all the dear friends who represent divine timing in my life, appearing at the right times, especially Jaime Adcock, Patricia Behmand, Kelly Etter Beilfuss, Duffy Bowden-Veazey, Alicia Forest, Dan Gremminger, Bradley Harding, Karen M. Jones, Al and Shelley McKittrick, Bill O'Brien, Delilah Ray, Pam Rogers, Kristin Troegle, and Deborah Eger Walsh. I give the biggest hug ever to my girlfriends Jean E. Sides, April Gorman, and Angela Hapka, for always providing just the right dose of motivation and/or procrastination during this book's process.

As I wrote this book, the sweet memories of Dee Dee Fields McKittrick, Becky Teter, John Makridakis, and Eva Stavroulakis danced lovingly in my heart.

I am deeply filled with appreciation for Dr. Jerry Lewis III and Dr. Roger Nathaniel, for their expertise and timely care. And thanks to my very special physical therapist, Terry Perez, for dynamically supporting my healing while I was writing this book.

The Big Island of Hawaii, where much of this material was conceived, provided endless seas of inspiration, and the waves continue to touch me, even though I now live so many miles away. *Mahalo nui loa* to Kristin Delgado, the Tutu's House Moms' Group, Jade McGaff, and Healer Extraordinaire Naya Rice.

I want to thank Alan Lightman, because his wonderful book *Einstein's Dreams* first introduced me to a poetic approach to time, and my inner clock was never the same.

And finally, my deepest appreciation extends to my husband, Anthony Makridakis, who introduced me to *Einstein's Dreams*...and to everything else that has mattered.

NOTES

1. WHAT IS TIME?

Page 10. *"Thus it is with time present"*: Jean Paul Richter, trans., *The Notebooks of Leonardo da Vinci* (Seattle: Pacific Publishing Studio, 2010), 215.

Page 10. *it also includes the near past and upcoming future*: William James, *The Principles of Psychology*, vol. 1 (New York: Cosimo, 2007), 609. First published in 1890.

Page 13. *oscillations of the "undisturbed" cesium atom*: James Jespersen and Jane Fitz-Randolph, *From Sundials to Atomic Clocks: Understanding Time and Frequency* (North Chelmsford: Courier Dover Publications, 1999), 110.

Page 14. *time is perceived about two and a half times faster than it was at age ten*: *Through the Wormhole*, "Does Time Exist?" season 2, episode 3 (S02E03), Science Channel, first aired June 23, 2011.

3. TIME AND RELATIVITY

Page 43. *the effects of altitude and gravitational force on time*: *Compton's Encyclopedia*, vol. 7, s.v. "Einstein, Albert (1879–1955)" (1989).

Page 44. *the Kappa effect can be seen* and *The Tau effect illustrates a similar phenomenon*: Jon E. Roecklein, *Elsevier's Dictionary of Psychological Theories* (London: Elsevier, 2006), 591.

Page 48. *clocks run faster at higher altitudes*: Edwin F. Taylor and John Archibald Wheeler, *Spacetime Physics: Introduction to Special Relativity* (New York: Macmillan, 1992), 133.

Page 51. *time wasn't standardized until 1884*: Barney Warf, *Time-Space Compression: Historical Geographies* (London: Psychology Press, 2008), 102.

Page 52. *Einstein's theory of relativity is popularly known through the equation E = mc²*: *Compton's Encyclopedia*, vol. 7, s.v. "Einstein, Albert (1879–1955)" (1989), 133.

Page 56. *"I want to have lived the width of it as well"*: Quoted in Anne Wilson Schaef, *Meditations for Women Who Do Too Much*, rev. ed. (New York: HarperCollins, 2004), 11.

Page 56. *There is no linguistic way to distinguish*: Harriet Wadeson, *Art Psychotherapy* (Hoboken, NJ: John Wiley and Sons, 2010), 52.

4. KRONOS AND KAIROS

Page 76. *"Now put the foundations under them"*: Henry David Thoreau, *Walden and Other Writings of Henry David Thoreau* (New York: Random House, 1965), 288.

Page 79. *"appealing to the higher emotions or to the aesthetic sense"*: *Merriam Webster's Collegiate Dictionary*, 10th ed., s.v. "numinous."

5. CREATING TIME THROUGH FLOW: TIME SIGHS WHEN YOU'RE HAVING FUN

Page 87. *when we are fully engaged with something outside ourselves*: Abraham Maslow, *Toward a Psychology of Being*, 2nd ed. (New York: Van Nostrand Reinhold, 1982), 80.

Page 87. *energized focus, full involvement, and success in the process of the activity*: Mihaly Csikszentmihalyi, *Finding Flow: The Psychology of Engagement with Everyday Life* (New York: Basic Books, 1998).

Page 90. *"tragically divided against ourselves"*: Martin Luther King Jr., *Strength to Love* (Cleveland: First Fortress Press, 1981), 51.

7. CREATING TIME THROUGH LOVE: TRAVELING AT THE SPEED OF LOVE

Page 114. *Richard Feynman's book* Six Not-So-Easy Pieces: Richard P. Feynman, *Six Not-So-Easy Pieces: Einstein's Relativity, Symmetry, and Space-Time* (Cambridge: Perseus Books, 1998), 128.

8. CREATING TIME THROUGH RITUAL: PUNCTUATING A DAY

Page 126. *a salute to Mother Earth and all her beauty*: Chief Jake Swamp, *Giving Thanks: A Native American Good Morning Message* (New York: Scholastic, 1997), 3.

Page 126. *the Balinese have about a dozen life cycle rites*: Leo Howe, *The Changing World of Bali: Religion, Society, and Tourism* (New York: Routledge, 2009), 58–60.

Page 126. *people often leave baskets of food on the ancestral burial ground*: Lois Siniako Webb, *Multicultural Cookbook of Life-Cycle Celebrations* (Santa Barbara, CA: ABC-CLIO, 2000), xlii.

Page 128. *"soil particles that have been dressed up in an icy cloak"*: Paul Douglas, *Restless Skies: The Ultimate Weather Book* (New York: Sterling, 2007), 41.

11. CREATING TIME THROUGH NEW MEASURES: LIFE IN A DAY

Page 161. *"the ability to select the precise moment for doing something for optimum effect"*: *Merriam Webster's Collegiate Dictionary*, 10th ed., s.v. "timing."

12. CREATING TIME THROUGH SYNCHRONICITY: TIME BESIDE TIME

Page 173. *He identified three types of synchronicity*: *The Collected Works of C. G. Jung*, vol. 8, *The Structure and Dynamics of the Psyche*, ed. Sir Herbert Read et al. (Princeton, NJ: Princeton University Press, 1970), 417.

Page 176. *"the man will fall off his bicycle"*: Robert Grudin, *Time and the Art of Living* (Cambridge: Harper & Row, 1982), 6.

13. CREATING TIME THROUGH VISUALIZATION: A GOOD, HARD LOOK AT "HARD TIMES"

Page 188. *"I have been tenderized"*: Becky Teter, ed., *TORCH: Tales of Remarkable Courage and Hope* (Dallas: Baylor Charles A. Sammons Cancer Center at Dallas, 1997), 52.

14. CREATING TIME THROUGH PERMISSION: THE RIGHT TO SET THE TIME RIGHT

Page 200. *write ourselves a "permission slip" to be creative*: SARK, *Living Juicy: Daily Morsels for Your Creative Soul* (Berkeley: Celestial Arts/Ten Speed Press, 1994).

16. CREATE YOUR OWN ARTsignments

Page 233. *a tree with mission, roles, and principles placed on it*: Stephen R. Covey, A. Roger Merrill, and Rebecca R. Merrill, *First Things First* (New York: Simon & Schuster, 1994), 125.

ILLUMINATING TIME WRAPS

Recommended Reading for
Positive Pockets of Time

*H*ere is a list of books that you can use to wrap yourself in positive pockets of time as you explore the subject in unconventional ways:

Badonsky, Jill. *The Awe-manac: A Daily Dose of Wonder*. Philadelphia: Running Press, 2008. This book looks at each day of the year through a richly creative lens; it is a wonderful daily ritual to expand your sense of possibility.

Csikszentmihalyi, Mihaly. *Finding Flow: The Psychology of Engagement with Everyday Life*. New York: Basic Books, 1998. Interesting reading for a comprehensive, fascinating study of "flow": what it is, and how to bring more of it into life.

Freeman-Zachery, Ricë. *Creative Time and Space: Making Room for Making Art*. Cincinnati: North Light Books, 2009. I serendipitously discovered this gem while in the final stages of editing my *Creating Time* manuscript. I love all the personal stories from artists, as they share how they manipulate their time and space.

Grudin, Robert. *Time and the Art of Living*. Cambridge: Harper & Row, 1982. This book is an intriguing series of essays on time; reading them is a meaningful meditation.

Jones, Karen M. *The Difference a Day Makes: 365 Ways to Change Your World in Just 24 Hours*. Novato, CA: New World Library, 2004. With a different world-changing idea for each day of the year, this book is a practical, hands-on guide for marking the days in a new way, through acts of service.

Katagiri, Dainin. *Each Moment Is the Universe: Zen and the Way of Being Time*. Boston: Shambhala, 2008. I enjoyed this collection of lectures by a Zen master, which collectively look at the subject of time through the practices of Zen Buddhism.

Lightman, Alan. *Einstein's Dreams*. New York: Vintage, 1993. This is a work of fictional vignettes imagining the fantastical time-themed dreams that Einstein had each night as he was developing the theory of relativity. It transformed me deeply, and I never looked at time the same way again. In fact, I consistently name this as my very favorite book.

Louden, Jennifer. *The Life Organizer: A Woman's Guide to a Mindful Year.* Novato, CA: New World Library, 2007. This book is designed to look like an organizer, but it is actually a very personal, practical guide to being more aware of your inner life. I used it religiously for a year and found that it helped me in ways I could never have imagined.

Paterniti, Michael. *Driving Mr. Albert: A Trip across America with Einstein's Brain.* New York: Bantam Dell, 2000. This memoir is a fun read, and I've included it in this list because it contains some excellent passages about time and perception.

Peat, F. David. *Synchronicity: The Bridge between Matter and Mind.* New York: Bantam, 1987. This is my favorite resource on the topic of synchronicity, and it is written in a way that satisfies both my inner spirit and my inner scientist.

Tolle, Eckhart. *The Power of Now: A Guide to Spiritual Enlightenment.* Novato, CA: New World Library, 1999. I see this book as the definitive guide to releasing the ego and bringing our consciousness to the presence of this moment.

CONTRIBUTORS

This book is graced by the stories and artwork of these amazing individuals. Please visit their websites, blogs, and Facebook pages to learn more about them and their wonderful talents. (Contact information was gathered in November 2011 and is accurate to best efforts at that time.)

SHERYL ALLEN offers playful, professional, savvy biz solutions for artists and women in small business. www.bodaciousbiz.com

CAITLIN ANDERSON finds ways to educate, inspire, transform, and create through art, workshops, and retreats. www.caitlinanderson.com

BRIAN ANDREAS is an artist and writer known worldwide for his lyrical, colorful stories. www.storypeople.com

JILL BADONSKY is an author, artist, and corporate dropout, and the creator of Kaizen-Muse Creativity Coaching. www.themuseisin.com

CHERYL BALL is a Co-Active and ARTbundance Coach, aspiring photographer, and book-arts artist living in San Francisco, California. cheryl@illumecoaching.com

MICHELLE BERLIN is a full-time artist and an ARTbundance Coach and Creativity Guide. www.LivingRightBrain.com

JAN BLOUNT created GratitudeAndCompany.com for those wishing to live more inspired, juicy, and enriched lives. GratitudeAndCompany.com

LANETTE BREEDT is a fun-loving creARTivity teacher, retreat presenter, and "timeless" artist from South Africa.

MARY BUTTERFIELD BROSHEAR loves creating and exploring the wondrous magic of art and life. www.paintcreatewrite.com

MARGUERITE BRYANT is a writer, multimedia artist, and ARTbundance Coach living in Northern California. artlovin1@suddenlink.net

ANGELA BYERS, a self-taught photographer, loves to dabble in all things creative and messy. www.visuallyoriented.blogspot.com

CALLIE CARLING is a creativity nurturer, ARTbundance Coach, and Magical Divine Heart Bliss Synergist. www.positivitybubbles.com

WILLIAM J. CHARLEBOIS enjoys writing and creating digital art on his iMac. www.wjcsdigitalworld.blogspot.com

VIOLETTE CLARK is a mixed media artist, author, and creative catalyst living in British Columbia, Canada. PurpleJuice.ca and www.violette.ca

LORI DANYLUK is passionate about living her purpose and helping others to do the same. www.ahandfulofinsight.wordpress.com

LEONIE DAWSON is the creator of GoddessGuideBook.com, a popular creativity, spirituality, and business blog for women. www.goddessguidebook.com

CHRISTINE DEJULIIS is an expressive arts advocate who believes in the artist in each of us. www.creativity-changes-everything.com

TARA DOUGLAS-SMITH is an education author and curriculum strategist who moonlights as an artist/poet.

LESLIE DUPONT is an ARTbundance Coach, editor, and writing teacher living in Tucson, Arizona. leslie@ArtellaLand.com

L'TANYA DURANTE is a writer, knitwear designer, and crafter living and creating in Durham, North Carolina. www.ltanyadurante.com

CARRIE FADEN is a mixed media artist, writer, inspirational speaker, and life coach. www.thebohemiancouch.blogspot.com

WENDY FEDAN is an illustrator and creator of her Create-A-Way business, living in Cleveland, Ohio. wfedan@earthlink.net

WOZ FLINT is an ARTbundance Coach, a writer, and one hip mama living in Albuquerque, New Mexico. www.cupokismet.wordpress.com

LARA GEACH, ARTbundance Coach and varied artist, creates in her forest studio in Perth, Australia. www.larageach.blogspot.com

ANGELA GEORGE is a self-esteem sculptor, jewelry artist, energy psychologist, and ARTbundance Coach. YourWellnessAngel@gmail.com

ATHENA GEORGE, abstract artist and ARTbundance Coach, is compassionately excited to help you discover the creative artist within. agpenson@yahoo.com

SHARON B. GORBERG is an artist, teacher, and time traveler living in the Boston area. sgorberg@gmail.com

DAN GREMMINGER is an art director, designer, illustrator, child at heart, and man about town. danno76@swbell.net

CHRIS HAMMER is an ARTbundance Coach, Rubenfeld Synergist, and lover of all things creative. Body-mind-matters.com

BRADLEY HARDING is an author, filmmaker, and entertainment journalist. bradlit@swell.net

ALLEGRA S. HARRINGTON creates sculpture to wear and photography in Norwalk, Connecticut. www.AllegraSHarrington.com

MARILYN HARRIS MILLS is a passionate, eccentric, and goofy full-time artist living in Ottawa, Canada. www.marilynharrismills.com

AMY HEIL is an enthusiastic mentor promoting artists at her store, BlueFish, on Martha's Vineyard. www.BlueFishMV.com

TAMMY HENSLEY is a graphic designer, fabric designer, and all-around artist. www.spoonflower.com/profiles/tammikins

MELANIE ADRIENNE HILL teaches and coaches others in creative processes for aligned and authentic living. www.MelanieAdrienneHill.com

GERRIE JOHNNIC loves to create with paper, rubber stamps, ink, and paint. www.Iwork4stamps2.blogspot.com

TERRY JORDAN is cofounder of EastWest Reiki Association, a community of practitioners sharing the benefits of self-care. www.eastwestreiki.org

KAREN KARSTEN, certified ARTbundance Coach, writer, and vivid dreamer, lives in St. Paul, Minnesota. ThinkYouCan.net

SUSAN ARIEL RAINBOW KENNEDY, aka SARK, is a bestselling author and artist who founded Planet SARK. www.PlanetSARK.com

ARTHISS KLIEVER, woodcut artist and paper crafter, supervises a neighborhood children's library in Dallas, Texas. www.launaslittlelibrary.com

JANET LAIRD is an ARTbundance Coach who combines art with WRAP (Wellness Recovery Action Planning). www.janetlaird.blogspot.com

TANYA LAURIN, an intuitive clairvoyant, offers Life Purpose Hand Analysis/Coaching, ARTbundance, and Laughter Yoga. www.holistictransformations.ca

SHELLEY LINDSEY is an ARTbundance Coach, mother, fiber artist, and clinical counselor residing in Cincinnati, Ohio. sal6547@yahoo.com

PEGGY LYNN is an artist, adventurer, and potentiality expert joyfully evoking all creative genius. www.PegLynnART.com

GWYN MALLOY is studying for her MA in counseling and living a creative life in Indianapolis, Indiana. gwynmalloy@ymail.com

TRISHA MARCY is the owner of Balanced Life Virtual Assistance and a lover of life. www.balancedlifeva.com

SHEILA MASSON is an astrologer, soul coach, and inspiring speaker living in rural Quebec. www.wisehearthealingarts.com

SUSAN MCLEAN, Michigan ARTbundance Coach and Creatively Fit Coach, engages creativity to enhance life sparkle. smcleancreativeenergysparkle@gmail.com

NANLEAH N. MICK is a Certified ARTbundance Coach/Practitioner and an Infinite Possibilities Certified Trainer. http://www.facebook.com/YourAdornment

DONNA MILLS, an artist, writer, and creativity midwife, helps her clients to birth their brilliant ideas. creativeclarity@me.com

K. LEE MOCK is an artist, educator, and healing spirit from Portsmouth, New Hampshire. k.leemock.art@gmail.com.

KELLY NOEL MORRISON is an ARTbundance Coach, awareness muse, and dynamic retreat creator. kellynoelmorrison@comcast.net and www.kellymorrison.byregion.net

PATRICIA J. MOSCA is an artist, writer, explorer of life, and work in progress. www.pjmosca.com

MAISEN MOSLEY is a survivor, mentor, and ARTbundance Coach, and the creator of Spirited Lady Living. www.spirited-lady-living.com

IRINA NASKINOVA is an ARTbundance Coach, dreamer, and lover of life, living in Bulgaria.

BHEKI NAYLOR is an artist, writer, and coach living in a sparkly, magic-filled cabin. www.bhekinaylor.com

DR. ANGELA KOWITZ OROBKO is an antibullying expert advocating kindness to create positive changes. www.HeartsThatCare.net

LUCINDA POLLIT is an ARTbundance Coach encouraging inner creative expression for authentic, joyful life transformations. www.lucindapollit.com

SIAN POPE is an intuitive coach and creative, living near Bristol, UK. sianpope@btinternet.com

JULIE PROCTOR is making meaning in her life through art, yoga, meditation, and journaling. kjpro@comcast.net

CHERYL RICHARDS, writer, artist, photographer, and time traveler, finds awe and inspiration in the everyday. www.cherylrichards.blogspot.com

DAWN RICHERSON helps visionaries and change agents to write, publish, and market their extraordinary books. www.creativerevolutions.com

SANDE ROBERTS is a personal and professional crisis prevention and intervention specialist. Unconventional approaches, amazing results. www.RealLifeSkillsWorkshops.com

JOZETTE RODRIGUEZ, a passion-preneur, creatively inspires and guides people toward discovering their innate divine wisdom. www.angeliqueawakening.com

YVONNE ROSE, a Toronto-based art psychotherapist and ARTbundance Coach, provides creative direction toward dream fulfillment. www.yvonnerose.com

VIVIAN SAKELLARIOU is an artist/teacher with an infinitely curious, creative spirit of exploration. kalitreeia@yahoo.com, www.flickr.com/photos/vastara

CHELLE SAMANIEGO, aka D-M-S, yearns to create and live simply for Christ. www.createforchrist.blogspot.com and www.christfollowingminimalist.wordpress.com

DANA SEBASTIAN-DUNCAN is an art therapist, creativity coach, and explorer/provider of enriching, creative, spiritual practices. www.creationonlocation.wordpress.com

RAE SHAGALOV coaches creatives who want to get really clear and focused on their business. HolySparks.org

JANET SHEPHERD is an ARTbundance Coach, artist, psychotherapist, and playful provocateur in Iowa City, Iowa. www.joyfullifedesign.com

JEAN E. SIDES is a devoted and fulfilled mom, wife, daughter, sister, friend, and volunteer.

SUSAN SCHIRL SMITH, RN, MSN, is a holistic nurse, ARTbundance practitioner, and creative dreamer. www.avalonhealingarts.com

CATHLEEN SPACIL, creator of Brain Be Happy, promotes wellness for those conquering mental illness and brain injury. www.brainbehappy.com

TERRI ST. CLOUD is a woman on a journey to find real. www.BoneSighArts.com

PAULA SWENSON is a creative catalyst, artist, writer, and nomad. www.creativespirals.com

TiCo is currently a designer (KnitfunctionalFamily.blogspot.com), ARTbundance Coach (PointofYouCoaching.com), and mixed media supply shop owner (www.passionknitlivingstudios.com).

DAVID WAGENFELD is an artist and Certified ARTbundance Coach living in Kalamazoo, Michigan. www.davidwagenfeld.com

JENNIFER WALLING founded FlyingArts, champions Art Adoptions, and enthusiastically supports all creative souls. www.flyingarts.com

SANDI WEDEMEIER is a professional psychic and ARTbundance Coach, artist, and writer. www.witandwisdomcoach.com

MIKELL Y. WORLEY is an ARTbundance Coach, artist, writer, and treasure hunter. www.hiddentreasuresinnature.com

INDEX

ABOUT THE AUTHOR

Marney K. Makridakis is the founder of ArtellaLand.com, the groundbreaking online community for artists, writers, and creative individuals. Since 2002, Artella has been a playland for creativity, full of innovative services that embrace the uniqueness of individuals, catalyzing unawakened inklings and inspirations to come alive and passionately thrive. Marney is a widely known voice in the creativity movement, frequently requested for interviews, guest columns, workshops, and speeches.

She is also the founder of the ARTbundance philosophy, an innovative approach of self-improvement through creativity, and the ARTbundance Certification Training Program (ACT), which trains people to use ARTbundance in professional venues, such as creativity coaching, teaching workshops, public speaking, and creating online environments. Both ACT and Artella's sister website, BusinessBohemia.com, are the result of her desire to help creatively minded people design a successful business rooted in true passion, personal joy, and creative meaning.

A graduate of Duke University, Marney lives in kairos time in Dallas, Texas, with her wonderful husband and their wise and adventurous young son, Kai. She names these things as being essential to her creative well-being: the color orange, poetic novels, singing loudly, daily naps, the love of a good man, and hero worship of Mary Poppins.

Visit the Enchanting Isles of Artella Land
to take your creativity on an amazing journey!

"Marney Makridakis's Artella Land is a creative fountain; the site just vibrates with joyful creative expression."
— SARK

"I don't know why Artella hasn't been nominated for a Pulitzer yet. Seriously, Artella has changed the scope of art and words forever."
— JILL BADONSKY

Get Inspired at Artella Land!

Join Artella Land's supportive, inspiring community of writers, artists, crafters, entrepreneurs, and creative spirits! Founded in 2002, Artella is full of inspiring resources that catalyze creative living and help make dreams come true, such as:

- Monthly e-magazines, including *The Art Journal Journey* and *Blissness Splash*.
- Hundreds of e-courses, virtual workshops, e-books, downloadable kits, and teleclasses for creative spirits.
- The Artella Member Ship, with a broad choice of luxury creativity cruise cabins …there's something for everyone!
- *Artella* magazine, the print magazine of words and art, where it all began.
- The renowned ARTbundance Certification Training program (ACT).
- NEW! Artella's Business Bohemia…a fantastical world where work feels like play!

Interested in Becoming an ARTbundance Coach or Practitioner?

The ARTbundance Certification Training Program (ACT) is a fourteen-week program that offers comprehensive training and turnkey business-building materials for using the ARTbundance Principles and ARTsignments in a variety of professional venues, including coaching, public speaking, teaching and leading workshops, and creating online learning environments. ACT is a joyful, immensely promising opportunity for those who would like to use their deep interests and passion for creativity to serve and inspire others through creative, satisfying work.

If you are interested in learning how ACT might help you to find and live your true creative calling, you can download your free ACT Welcome Pack, including downloads of ARTbundance classes, the *Audio ACTimonials* audio program with real ACT graduates sharing their experiences, and the "Is ACT for Me?" workbook, with fun, innovative ARTsignments to help you determine if ACT might be the next step on your creative path.

To download your free ACT Welcome Pack, go to:

www.ArtellaLand.com/ACT-pack.html

To learn more about ACT and request an application
when our next session is announced, go to:

www.ArtellaLand.com/ACT-info.html

NEW WORLD LIBRARY is dedicated to publishing books and other media that inspire and challenge us to improve the quality of our lives and the world.

We are a socially and environmentally aware company, and we strive to embody the ideals presented in our publications. We recognize that we have an ethical responsibility to our customers, our staff members, and our planet.

We serve our customers by creating the finest publications possible on personal growth, creativity, spirituality, wellness, and other areas of emerging importance. We serve New World Library employees with generous benefits, significant profit sharing, and constant encouragement to pursue their most expansive dreams.

As a member of the Green Press Initiative, we print an increasing number of books with soy-based ink on 100 percent postconsumer-waste recycled paper. Also, we power our offices with solar energy and contribute to nonprofit organizations working to make the world a better place for us all.

Our products are available
in bookstores everywhere.
For our catalog, please contact:

New World Library
14 Pamaron Way
Novato, California 94949

Phone: 415-884-2100 or 800-972-6657
Catalog requests: Ext. 50
Orders: Ext. 52
Fax: 415-884-2199
Email: escort@newworldlibrary.com

To subscribe to our electronic newsletter, visit
www.newworldlibrary.com